EVIDENCE

Evidence

Book 1 of the Search for Truth Series

Ruth Chesney

JOHN RITCHIE LTD
CHRISTIAN PUBLICATIONS

40 Beansburn, Kilmarnock, Scotland

ISBN-13: 978 1 910513 36 1

This is a work of fiction. The characters, incidents and dialogues are products of the author's imagination and are not to be construed as real. Any resemblance to actual events or persons, living or dead, is entirely coincidental.

Typeset by John Ritchie Ltd., Kilmarnock
Printed by Bell & Bain, Glasgow

In memory of my precious friend, Louise McNeill (1984-2011), who loved books every bit as much as I do, and was the very first person to cheer on my attempts at writing.

'The memory of the just is blessed…'
(Proverbs 10:7 KJV)

Contents

Preface

Welcome to my first book! The story is set in Northern Ireland, where I was born and have always lived. It is a beautiful little corner of the world and holds a special place in my heart. However, for the purposes of the story, I have made some changes to the geography, so, while some of the places are based on real locations, you will search in vain for Cherryhill Farm. I have also taken the liberty of moving the date of the main agricultural show to July. I trust this will not cause any undue distress!

A book like this is a team effort and I'm very much indebted to the following people for their invaluable assistance and advice: Margaret Moore, Phillip Moore, Eunice Wilkie, David Williamson, Linda Kissick, Joanne Grattan and my teenage reader, Beth Herbison, whose comments made me smile and warmed my heart. I couldn't have done it without you all. If any errors remain, I am solely to blame. Thanks, also, to Alison Banks, General Manager of John Ritchie Ltd, for agreeing to take a risk with this new and untested author, and to Pete Barnsley, of Creative Hoot, for creating such a wonderful cover. And last, but not least, a special thank you to my husband, Samuel – your confidence in me, your encouragement and quiet strength is appreciated more than words can say.

Chapter One

"Seb! *Seb!* SEEEEBBB!" A shrill shriek pierced the air. "Come downstairs *this instant,* you wicked boy!"

The boy in question groaned and buried his head under his pillow. It smelled comforting, his refuge in the domestic storms that often rocked the small, grimy house he called home.

Footsteps sounded on the creaky stairs, accompanied by huffs and puffs.

"SEB! I'm going to drag you out by your ugly lug and give you what for if you don't make a move *right now!*"

Wheezing and sweating, the large form of his gran lumbered into the room on puffy, swollen ankles. Seb pulled his head from under the pillow and darted to the window, narrowly missing a swipe from her pudgy hand.

"Right, you ungrateful wretch," she growled. "Where did you put them?" She fixed him with a dark-eyed glare. *The Witch,* his friends called her. Stick-straight, black-dyed hair, which usually stuck out in all directions, a beak of a nose and even a hairy wart on her chin.

All that was missing was the broomstick.

The black cat slunk into the room behind her.

"Where did I put what?" he asked cheekily.

The dark eyes ignited with rage. "You insolent *brat!*" She shook a fist and advanced around the end of the bed. Seb saw his opportunity for escape as he leapt over the bed towards the door. Kicking the cat out of the way, he fled down the stairs and out of the house into the dull, drizzly June evening, slamming the door behind him.

Down behind the houses ran the railway. Seb slipped through a hole in the dilapidated fence and sat with his back pressed against the faded artistic graffiti left by a previous generation of youths. He often came here to escape. Gran would never find him here and even if she did, she would never be able to climb through the fence. He pulled up the hood of his grey sweatshirt and tugged the cuffs over his hands.

After a while, he pulled Gran's cigarettes out of his pocket and looked at them – 'Smoking Kills', the packaging proclaimed. He shrugged. Gran was ancient and she hadn't died yet, he thought, although she coughed so hard sometimes he wondered if she might not drop down dead there and then.

He fished around in his other pocket for the lighter he had grabbed from the hall table on his way out the door. After a few downward swipes of his thumb on the metal disc he managed to produce a steady flame.

A train sounded in the distance. Seb stuck the lighter back in his pocket and pressed himself against the fence. He could see the train lights approaching. As it whooshed past he caught glimpses of people inside – men in suits reading large, boring newspapers, women on their smartphones, and, in the last carriage, a fleeting snapshot of a family who appeared to be having some sort of a picnic, their faces wreathed in smiles. The image lingered, the lights faded into the distance and the cold draught enveloped him.

He pulled the lighter out of his pocket once more, this time tearing the clear plastic from the cigarette packet. He'd never tried smoking before, but this was his opportunity. Copying what he'd seen Gran and Dad do countless times, he lifted one out, popped the end in his mouth and went to light it. *Smoking kills.* His hand trembled. He didn't particularly want to die.

"Seb, there's nothing after death. We die; that's it," his dad's voice echoed in his head.

He put his thumb on the lighter.

"Death is not the end!" This time, the voice of a radio preacher. A day which was etched in his memory. His mother had burst into tears and his father had mocked her and shouted at her, before finally grabbing her by the hair and shoving her against the wall. It was one of a number of ugly scenes he tried to suppress.

Stuffing the image in the darkest recesses of his mind, he succeeded in lighting the cigarette. Taking a long draw, he waited for the satisfying feeling he always saw on Gran's and Dad's faces. No satisfying feeling came - only a horrible, nauseating, choking sensation. He coughed and spat. Trying again, he breathed a little less deeply, but still the nausea persisted and strengthened. Staggering to his feet, he threw up in the bushes.

Grinding the cigarette out with the heel of his trainer, he made for home. It was getting cold and he just wanted to go to bed after the experience he'd had. Smoking wasn't all it was made out to be. And smoking kills.

As he put his hand on the door handle, he could hear the blare of a football match coming from the TV inside. If he was quiet he could make his way upstairs to his room without being seen. Pushing gently, he opened the door. His mum was standing at the foot of the stairs, her pale blue care assistant's uniform hanging loosely on her slight frame.

"Where on earth have you been?!" she exclaimed. "Gran said you'd stolen something from her and ran off. You've been away for ages!"

"Nowhere much," Seb grunted, as he tried to push past.

Mum caught him by his shoulder. "Seb..." She stopped. Leaning across, she sniffed his pale blond hair. "Seb! Please don't tell me you've been smoking!"

Seb grunted again.

"Have you?" she persisted.

"NO!" Seb lied, as he tried to wriggle free from her surprisingly firm grasp.

"What's going on out there?" Dad's voice bellowed from the living room.

"Seb was smoking!" Mum hauled him into the room.

Dad was sprawled on the sofa, stained blue t-shirt taut over his large belly. He laughed. "And how did you manage?" he asked. "Bet you were sick. A weakling like you wouldn't be able to smoke like a man."

Seb glared at him.

Dad threw back his head and roared. "Poor wee Mummy's boy," he jeered. "Can't even manage one measly cigarette!"

"That is *enough!*" Mum choked out through gritted teeth. "Do you really want Seb to turn out like you?"

Dad launched to his feet, raising a large fist. "And just what's wrong with me, you-"

"Mind your language!" Mum spat, interrupting him before he could utter whatever foul word he'd been about to say.

Seb slipped out of the room and upstairs. Throwing himself on the bed, he could hear the argument continuing in the room below.

"Who are you to tell me to mind my language?" roared Dad. "I don't know what your problem is anyway. You were good fun until *he* came along, and then you went all goody-goody on me."

"I *told* you! I don't want to bring Seb up like this. I want him to go to church and hear how he can be saved..."

"SHUT UP!" Dad bellowed. "If you mention *saved* to me once more I'll kill you!" The front door slammed, and in the sudden calm a soft weeping came from below.

Seb could hardly remember a time when his parents didn't fight. Lately the fights had become more frequent. And Dad was drinking more. Sometimes he was out all night and slept all day, especially when there wasn't any work on the building sites, which was nearly all the time now. Mum worked long hours to make ends meet, and Gran came to stay with him when he came home from school until Mum came back each evening.

Shoving back the covers, he kicked off his shoes and got into bed. He hadn't done his homework, but it was no big deal. Much to his teachers' frustration, homework was treated as optional by the pupils at his school; he'd only be one among a number. And with just one week of school to go before the summer holidays, even the teachers had given up by now.

The phone's shrill tone pierced the morning air. Seb stirred. 5:45am, his bedside clock read. The ringing stopped, and he dozed off again. A few minutes later Mum burst into his room, running a brush through her tangled yellow hair, the dark roots a stark contrast.

"Gran has collapsed," she said. "I've phoned the ambulance and I'm going with her to the hospital. You'll have to get your own breakfast this morning. Make sure you're at school on time."

With that, she was gone.

Seb didn't bother going to school. He awoke again at 10am and found an opened box of soft cornflakes. There was no milk in the fridge, but he found a carton of orange yoghurt past its use by date. Grabbing a bowl from the draining rack, he filled it with the cornflakes and yoghurt. Not his favourite combination, but he was hungry, so it was better than nothing. He took the heaped bowl into the living room and turned on the TV. Nothing but home improvement programmes and chat shows. He searched for the recorded items. Finding a film his dad had recorded, he settled down to watch.

An hour into the film, he heard the key turn in the lock. Grabbing the remote, he turned the TV off and looked around to see where to hide, but it was too late.

Mum looked into the room. "Seb!" she exclaimed. "Why aren't you at school?"

Seb shrugged.

Mum sighed. "What am I going to do with you?"

"How's The Witch?" he asked.

"Seb! That's not nice. You shouldn't call your grandmother

names." Mum sighed again. "Gran isn't well," she continued. "They haven't ruled out lung cancer. She's to have tests. Whatever it is, it isn't going to work out for her to stay with you over the summer holidays." Mum sank onto the sofa and rubbed her forehead.

"But I don't need looked after! I'm not a baby!" Seb protested. "And sure I'm on my own today and I've managed fine."

"And just what were you watching when I came in?" Mum asked, raising her eyebrows suspiciously at him.

Seb looked away.

"I hope it wasn't something your dad recorded!"

Seb bit his lip and kicked at the leg of the coffee table.

Mum briefly closed her eyes and sighed. She almost looked as if she was in pain. "Anyway," she continued, "you can't spend all day in front of the TV. I was wondering if Matt and Karen would take you for the summer."

"What?!" Seb sat bolt upright. "Uncle Matt and Aunt Karen? But I don't even know them! And don't they live on a farm? Farms *smell!*"

"You get used to the smell," replied Mum, unearthing the portable phone from a pile of newspapers, magazines and biscuit wrappers on the coffee table. She began to punch in a number she found in a small diary in her handbag.

Seb could hear the faint ringing tone from the phone, and he held his breath. Then a distant male voice. "Hello?"

"Matt?" Seb's mum said. "It's Julie...I know, it's been a long time...yes, we're fine...Seb's okay...actually, that's what I'm phoning about..."

Mum got up, phone still to her ear, and left the room, closing the door behind her.

Seb fell back against the seat. If Uncle Matt agreed, this would be his very worst summer ever. A farm. Miles from town. And with Uncle Matt and Aunt Karen. Christians! Then he remembered - Dad loathed Christians...! Seb smiled. Dad would never agree to him going there for the summer.

"Matt and Karen's? No way!" Dad declared later that day. "They'll fill his head full of religious nonsense and it'll be the ruination of him."

Mum bit her lip. She looked like she very much wanted to say something.

"And why can't he stay by himself? He's old enough," Dad continued.

"Alan, he isn't an adult. He can't be trusted. He skipped school today and was watching one of your films when I came home."

Dad smirked. "Ha! Maybe we'll make a man out of him yet! No, Julie, he's not going there. He'll be fine on his own. Not another word about it."

Chapter Two

Seb threw down his black school sports bag, slumped onto the fuzzy blue seat of the early morning, country-bound train, and stared moodily out the window at the hustle and bustle of the platform. His mother lifted the bag and stowed it into the overhead storage. She slipped into the seat across the grey plastic table from Seb.

"You'll enjoy it," she said to him.

Seb said nothing in reply. He was still angry at having been made to go to Uncle Matt and Aunt Karen's after all. If only he hadn't played with the lighter in the house. If only the sofa hadn't caught fire. If only he'd had the presence of mind to put it out instead of running away in a panic. If only...

Unfortunately, once Dad saw the ruined living room, and, more specifically, the ruined 42-inch screen TV, all hope of Seb staying at home over the summer vanished quicker than the old, ugly, green sofa when the flames caught hold. He was fortunate the postman had noticed the smoke through the window and the house hadn't burned down. Spending the summer with 'religious bigots' was appropriate punishment, as far as Dad was concerned.

The train moved off, slowly at first. He could see a suited young man running towards the train, then slowing and shaking his head as he realised the train was leaving. *Too late,* thought Seb, wishing he could swap places. He'd hardly ever been out of Belfast in his life, and 'Matt, Karen, Lavinia and Martha' were only names on a Christmas card, which was propped up until Dad came home, and then was torn into tiny pieces and flung into the bin. Seb supposed it didn't help that there was always some sort of Bible verse on the card. Something like, 'Christ Jesus came into the world to save sinners'. He'd always wondered if there really had been such a person as Christ Jesus, and if He really came into the world, or if He was someone just like Santa Claus, someone who the adults always pretended was real, but was totally made up.

Dad always scoffed. "There's no such person," he often told Seb. "God doesn't exist. Everything started with a big bang." He'd told Seb so many times that he believed him now. He didn't see much to convince him otherwise anyway. "No intelligent person believes in God anymore," his biology teacher at school told the class. "Scientific evidence shows that we are products of evolution and the universe began with the Big Bang."

The train passed through a tunnel and the view of metal fences and overgrown shrubbery was replaced for an instant by his scowling reflection. Seb was actually going to stay with a family who didn't care about scientific evidence. He was dreading it. He tried to imagine what they would be like. Long, sad faces with droopy eyes. Like those religious pictures he'd seen hanging in Mrs Maguire's house when Mum used to go every week to clean it back when he was seven or eight. This was going to be the longest summer of his life.

Blinking, he looked out the window again. He could see the back of the terraced houses of his street. Some yards tidy, others overgrown and strewn with junk and children's toys. He recognised the stretch of graffiti where he'd taken his first fateful puff of a cigarette. He could have got used to it if they hadn't banned him from having a lighter and sent him away. He might have made his father proud, for once.

The houses soon gave way to industrial buildings, to larger houses with gardens, and then green fields. The farther they travelled from the city, the more Mum seemed to unwind. Seb sneaked a glance at her. She was actually smiling! He couldn't remember the last time Mum had smiled. She caught his gaze and reached across to squeeze his arm. He shrugged away from her touch.

"You'll enjoy it," she said again.

"Don't know what makes you think that," Seb muttered.

"Matt and Karen are decent people," she went on, "and Lavinia, your cousin, is around your age."

"What kind of a name is that?" Seb scoffed.

"She's called after her grandmother, Matt's mother," replied Mum. "You know Karen and I are sisters. We didn't grow up on a farm, but we did live in the country. I had a great childhood. Matt's uncle left him Cherryhill Farm and he moved back from Scotland after university to take it over. He's done well with it. It's a good opportunity for you to experience another way of life. But Seb, please be good, do what you're told and be polite, for goodness' sake. Don't let me down."

"Like you never let me down," Seb muttered sarcastically.

The smile disappeared and Mum's face crumpled. She pulled a wrinkled tissue from the pocket of her hooded sweatshirt.

Seb rolled his eyes and turned to look out the window again.

As the train slowed to a stop Mum stood up.

"Come on," she smiled, all evidence of her earlier tears gone, "we're almost there!"

Seb dragged himself to his feet, pulled the bag from the storage rack and followed her down the short aisle to the nearest door. His stomach was starting to churn. He was being sent to stay for two whole months with people he didn't know, miles from anywhere. Would they like him? Would he have to go to church? What would he do all day? Surely he wouldn't be expected to help! Would he be able to stand the smell? He looked at his feet. What about his new trainers? Would they get ruined with mud? What had Mum told

Uncle Matt and Aunt Karen about him? They likely thought he was a spoiled city brat. A no-good waster, like his dad. A...

Mum suddenly grabbed his arm. Seb jumped. He hadn't been concentrating where they were walking and he looked up to see a tall, dark haired man striding towards them, his face wreathed in smiles. He wore blue jeans and a navy body warmer over a checked shirt, sleeves rolled up to the elbows to reveal strong, muscular arms.

"Julie," he said, as he reached forward to give Seb's mum a brief hug. "Good to see you. It's been too long."

Mum looked away, biting her lip. For an instant the familiar lines returned to her forehead, then she smiled. "I know, Matt, and I'm sorry."

"We were so glad you got in touch," he replied. "You know we meant it when we said we'd always be here." He turned to Seb. "And you must be Seb!" His huge, rough hand engulfed Seb's in a hearty handshake. "We're delighted you're coming to stay with us. And Vinnie is ecstatic! She's so excited about having company over the summer."

Seb nodded. He felt in awe of this giant-like man.

"Now, let's get going." Matt led the way out to the car park. Seb looked around for their means of transportation, expecting maybe a tractor, or a dirty, straw-covered vehicle of some description. He was pleasantly surprised when Matt stopped beside a huge, black, shiny, chrome-embellished pickup truck.

"Cool!" Seb exclaimed, his excitement momentarily sweeping away his belligerent attitude. He ran his hand across the chrome bar at the front. "I thought we'd be going in a tractor."

Matt threw back his head and laughed. "You'll see plenty of tractors," he said, "but they're only used for farm work, not for picking up special guests from the station! Come on, hop in!"

The journey to Cherryhill Farm seemed to last forever. Much as Seb loved the ride in the amazing truck, they seemed to make so many turns on narrow roads that he couldn't have found his way back if he'd tried. He'd never seen so many fields and so few houses. And no shops at all! Where did they get their groceries? Surely they couldn't grow *everything*, could they?

Finally, Uncle Matt indicated left and slowed. "We're nearly home, Seb," he called over his shoulder.

Seb could see a tree-lined lane leading up a slight incline towards a symmetrical ivy-covered house. The door in the centre was flanked by two windows on either side, with upstairs windows directly above those downstairs, and another window in the centre above the door. There was a small garden at the front, neatly fenced, with a few trees and bushes, bright with coloured blooms. Beyond the house lay a collection of grey outbuildings, and he could see a bright blue tractor parked beside one.

Uncle Matt swung the truck around to the back of the house,

and Seb heard the sound of a dog barking. He looked around and saw a large black and white collie running from the direction of the outbuildings. Uncle Matt pulled up beside a small red car, and stepped out. The collie ran up and pressed her head against his leg. He reached down to rub her ears. "Well, Jess-girl," he said, "we've visitors today."

Seb climbed out of the truck, and Jess sniffed his toes, then gazed up at him inquisitively.

"You can stroke her," said Matt, "she's good with people. Not much of a guard dog, is our Jess!"

Seb reached out and patted her soft black head. She shuffled closer.

"She likes you," smiled Uncle Matt. "Come on, time for spoiling Jess later. She'd have you standing there all day if it was up to her!"

He opened the back door. "Karen! Girls! We're here!"

As Seb stepped into a small porch, the door to the left was suddenly flung open. A petite lady, brown hair pulled back in a ponytail and wearing a red apron and a warm smile appeared, with two girls - one a teenager and the other a lot younger - close behind.

"Come in! You're so welcome!" the lady, who he assumed must be Aunt Karen, exclaimed. "And Julie…" she broke off to give her sister a tight hug. "I'm so glad to see you again. I've missed you so much." Seb glanced at his mum, who was crying yet again.

"I'm Lavinia," the older girl spoke, turning his attention from the tearful reunion going on behind him, "but most people call me Vinnie. You must be Seb. You're going to love it here. A farm is totally the best place *ever* to live. I'm going to show you my heifer, we're taking her to the show this year and I'm sure she'll come first in her class, and you'll have to learn how to do the milking and help with the silage and... *Oh!*" Her dark eyes danced and she leaned forward, hands outstretched. "Jess is having pups soon! I can't *wait!* Summer is my favourite time!"

Aunt Karen chuckled at her daughter. She had one arm around Mum, who was frantically rubbing her eyes and nose with the now-mutilated tissue. "Lavinia! You can educate Seb on the virtues of summertime on a farm later! This is Martha," she went on, putting her other hand on the little girl's blonde curls. "She's four. Say 'hi', Martha."

Martha gave a shy smile. "Hi," she whispered.

"Now, come through to the kitchen and we'll have a cuppa. Julie doesn't have long before she has to get the train back."

They all entered a large kitchen which stretched the whole width of the house. The room had two distinct sections – the far end, the one towards the front of the house, had a selection of cosy sofas and armchairs angled towards an open fire, while the part in which Seb was now standing had a large pale blue painted wooden table in the centre, and a large black Aga stove directly opposite.

Aunt Julie directed Seb towards one of the sofas, and he sank into the plush leather. A coffee table in front had a neat pile of magazines, topped by a large black leather-bound Bible. Seb looked away. He couldn't understand how such welcoming, friendly people could be deceived so badly. They certainly weren't how he imagined them to be anyway. Why did they seem so happy? Mum and Dad rarely smiled and the lines around Mum's eyes were worry lines, not laughter ones like Aunt Karen's.

Lavinia sprawled onto the armchair beside the sofa.

"Have you ever been on a farm before?" she asked.

Seb shook his head. "No," he muttered.

"Seriously?!" Lavinia exclaimed. "You don't know what you've been missing."

Seb was starting to get a bit fed up with his cousin's obsession about her farm, so he pulled out his phone and scrolled through the latest photos and updates of his friends' lives. He'd already seen everything new on the train on the way here, but acting as if he were preoccupied gave him a welcomed reprieve. Just as he felt he had seen enough pictures of what he was missing back in Belfast, Aunt Karen called them over to the table.

"Have this seat, Seb," she smiled, patting the wooden back of one of the chairs. He sat down and surveyed the table. It was laden with different types of bread, some butter and two pots of jam, a plate with some cake, and a three-tiered stand crammed with buns and biscuits. It all looked delicious, and Seb was starting to feel ravenous.

It didn't take long for everyone to find a seat. Seb looked around. Why was no one reaching for something to eat? He lifted a hand to help himself to a particularly tempting piece of cake.

"Seb, in this house we give God thanks for our food before we eat, so we'll just pray and then you can tuck into whatever you'd like."

Seb snatched his hand back and looked around to see all eyes on him.

"I don't believe in God," he blurted out.

"*Seb!*" Mum scolded, her face burning with embarrassment.

"Well, I don't," he shrugged. "Dad says religion is a crutch for the weak." He narrowed his eyes and looked defiantly at Uncle Matt.

To his surprise, Uncle Matt smiled at him. "Seb, we'll talk about this again. For now, we're giving thanks for this food. We're grateful for it, and we want to thank God, regardless of your beliefs, or lack of!" With that, he bowed his head and closed his eyes, and the rest followed suit.

Seb defiantly lifted his chin and opened his eyes wide, but he couldn't help hearing what Uncle Matt was supposedly telling God – thanking Him for bringing Seb and Julie to Cherryhill safely and asking God to 'bless Seb' and to give Julie a safe journey back, as well as thanking Him for the 'delicious food' from God's 'gracious hand'.

Finally he said, "Amen," and everyone lifted their heads and started to chat. Aunt Karen held out the plate of cake to Seb and he chose a piece, but strangely he didn't feel just quite so hungry now. Uncle Matt's short prayer echoed in his mind – bless Seb... bless Seb... bless Seb. Whatever did he mean?

Chapter Three

After everyone had eaten their fill, Aunt Karen directed them over to the sitting area.

"Leave the dishes, Julie," she said to Seb's mum. "We've years of chat to catch up on."

Seb's mum gave her a sad smile. "There isn't much to tell," she replied, but set the mugs down anyway and took a seat in a wooden rocking chair with a blue tartan rug draped over the back.

Lavinia leaned forward. "Want to come and see round the farm?" she asked Seb.

He shrugged and got to his feet. It'd be better than hanging around being bored by old-people chat anyway.

Lavinia stopped by the door to pull on a thick pair of socks and green wellies.

"Do you have wellies?" she asked Seb.

"Wellies?" he echoed. "Why would I need wellies?" He rolled his eyes in disgust.

Lavinia giggled. "Oh, I forgot you're a tow... em, a person from the town," she finished.

Seb wasn't quite sure what she'd been about to say. He didn't think he really wanted to know.

"Come on, follow me," she said, then whistled to Jess. Jess stood up from the spot where she was sunning herself under the kitchen windowsill and trotted obediently to Lavinia, who stroked her ears. Jess sank onto Lavinia's feet and closed her eyes in rapture.

"Her pups are due in a few weeks," Lavinia said. "We might keep one this time. You can help me choose."

Seb grunted. He had no experience with dogs, apart from watching the neighbour's pit bull terrier over the fence. It bared its teeth and growled at him, especially if he teased it. He figured it was kept for fighting.

Lavinia straightened and gave Jess a final pat. "We'll go to the milking parlour first," she said.

As they walked across the yard towards the sheds, Seb became aware of a distinctive odour. He wrinkled his nose. "That's disgusting!" he exclaimed.

Lavinia looked at him, puzzled. "What is?" she asked.

"That smell," he said, shuddering.

Lavinia stopped and inhaled deeply. "I don't smell anything," she told him. "Well, maybe the smell of cows, but it's not very strong, and I like it – it's the smell of home! Wait until Dad's spreading slurry, then you'll know all about smells!" She giggled.

Seb looked away. Lavinia was starting to get on his nerves.

They reached the milking parlour and climbed up the metal steps. Lavinia slid back the red door. It was quite dark inside and the room they'd stepped into was almost completely taken up with a large, shiny tank. Lavinia patted the side of it. "This is where the milk is stored and cooled until it's collected," she said, then disappeared around the side, flicked on a light switch, and slid back another small door.

Seb followed Lavinia and found himself in another room. In the centre of this long, narrow room was what Seb immediately thought of as a trench, running towards the far end of the room, and about four feet deep. On either side there were two long passages with gates at the end nearest to where Seb was standing. Above the trench, twenty large glass jars and a myriad of pipes of different colours and sizes were suspended from the ceiling. Lavinia hopped down the steps, and waited for Seb to follow.

"This is where we stand to milk the cows," she told him. "The cows stand at each side and we can milk twenty at once with these." She tapped one of the sets of pipes which had four cylindrical metal ends.

It didn't make any sense to Seb, but he nodded anyway. He figured it wasn't a good time to admit that he had imagined the milking parlour would consist of a three-legged stool and a bucket.

Lavinia smiled. "You'll have to see it in action later," she said. "I hope you brought some old clothes with you - the cows aren't potty trained!" She giggled again.

Seb had no idea what she was talking about, but she had already hopped back up the steps and was making her way outside again.

He followed her to a shed where straw and sawdust was kept for bedding the animals and then they visited the calf house. "There are no calves yet," she said, "but you might get to see some before you go home at the end of the summer."

The end of the summer! Seb shuddered, and kicked at a small stone. It was starting to sink in. This farm, with its smells, its strange machinery, the prayers, and this over-talkative cousin, was going to be his home for the next two months. Sensing Lavinia looking at him, he glanced up to see a mixture of concern and bewilderment on her usually smiling face.

"What is it, Seb?" she asked. "Don't you want to be here?"

"No, I don't!" he exclaimed viciously. "I've been sent here out of the way because Mum and Dad don't think I'm old enough to look after myself. I'd much rather be back in Belfast where there are things to do, and not be stuck away out in the middle of nowhere being bored silly and having religion rammed down my throat. And having to listen to you nattering on all day as well!" He looked away from the hurt expression on Lavinia's face, and continued on. "You're all such a bunch of goody-goodies, all happy and smiling, like you're not even in the real world! Well, not everyone has it so good, you know." He stopped, suddenly remembering that he was trying to convince his cousin that his life in Belfast was what he really wanted.

Lavinia sighed. "Let's get back to the house," she said softly. "Your mum will be leaving soon."

Neither spoke on the short walk back. Seb sat down on the back step and Jess pressed against him. Lavinia prised off her wellies in the porch and padded into the kitchen in her socks. The two women were sitting on the sofa, both with their heads bowed. As they lifted their heads she could see Aunt Julie had been crying. She quickly wiped her eyes and smiled at Lavinia. "Nice walk?" she asked.

Lavinia nodded.

"Good," Julie said, then turned to Karen again. "I'm so glad that Seb can get away from home for a while. I thought it wasn't going to happen as Alan is dead set against the Bible, and Seb is just soaking up all he tells him. I can't make any impression on him at all. Maybe here he'll finally accept what I've always hoped he would. It's too late for me, but Seb's young."

"Julie," Karen spoke, "it's not too late for you. God is still offering you forgiveness. He loves you, and gave His Son to die for you; you just need to accept Him."

Julie smiled sadly and shook her head. "I'd better get going," she said. "I don't want to miss the train."

Karen gave her a hug. "I'm praying for you," she whispered. "And don't worry about Seb; we'll look after him like he's our own."

Uncle Matt insisted that Seb come with him to take his mum to the station. He figured another ride in the truck would be more fun than listening to the chatter of his cousin, although she didn't come out to wave them off, and he wondered if she was still speaking to him. *Doesn't matter,* he thought. *I don't care what she thinks of me.*

At the station he had to endure a hug from his mum, along with a list of instructions about being good, not being cheeky and listening to Uncle Matt. He rolled his eyes. If she was so worried about him, why was she leaving him here?

On the way back to the truck, Uncle Matt patted Seb on the shoulder. "I'm glad you're here," he grinned. "I get a bit outnumbered with all those ladies at home!"

They climbed in and Matt started the engine. The truck roared to life. Seb couldn't help the grin which spread over his face. If his friends could see him now... "How fast can this thing go?" he asked.

Uncle Matt threw back his head and laughed. "This model is usually 175bhp, but this one is remapped to 209bhp." He lowered his voice and winked, "It can go pretty fast!"

Seb grinned back.

Uncle Matt pulled out of the station and headed towards the centre of town.

"Where are we going?" Seb asked.

"I need to pick up a few bits and pieces for Karen, and then I thought we'd head out to Harvey's and get you all kitted out for living on a farm."

Seb frowned at him. "You mean, like, wellies and stuff?" he asked.

"Exactly!" Uncle Matt nodded. "You can't bring the cows in in those fancy trainers!" He pointed at Seb's feet.

"What makes you think I'll be helping bring the cows in?" Seb glared at him.

Uncle Matt shrugged. "Everyone helps out," he said. "You'll get bored awfully quick if you don't." He paused and a twinkle appeared in his eye. "You might actually find you like farming!"

In an hour they were ready to leave for home. While at the supermarket Matt had thrown two pairs of jeans, a few t-shirts, thick socks and a couple of sweatshirts into the trolley. At Harvey's, the agricultural supply store, he bought him wellies and a pair of brown dealer boots. These clothes were all so different from what he usually wore, but if Uncle Matt wanted to waste his money on 'farmer clothes' for Seb, that was his choice.

Once they reached the national speed limit at the edge of town, Uncle Matt pressed down on the accelerator and pulled away. Seb could feel the thrust of every bit of that 209bhp pushing him back in his seat.

"Wow!" Seb exclaimed. "This is awesome!"

Uncle Matt grinned. He flipped on the CD player and the cab was filled with upbeat country guitar music.

> *Would you be free from your burden of sin?*
>> *There's power in the blood, power in the blood!*
> *Would you o'er evil a victory win?*
>> *There's wonderful power in the blood!*

Uncle Matt joined in, tapping his hand on the steering wheel in time to the music.

Seb had never heard such strange lyrics before. *Power in the blood?* What blood? Why would there be power in blood? This was like nothing he'd ever heard before.

As the song ended, Uncle Matt looked across at him. Seeing his bewilderment, he smiled.

"Ever heard that one before?" he asked.

"Never," Seb admitted. "What was it all about?"

"It's about the power in the blood of the Lord Jesus Christ. 'The blood of Jesus Christ His Son,' that is, God's Son, 'cleanses us from all sin.'"

Seb rolled his eyes. "So it's a religious song."

"Seb," Uncle Matt spoke, "what exactly is it you have against 'religion', as you call it?"

"My dad says it's a crutch, that there is no God, and when we die, that's it."

"And what do you think?" Matt asked.

"The same as my dad," Seb shrugged.

"Have you ever thought about it for yourself?" Uncle Matt asked kindly.

"Why would I need to?" replied Seb. "I've never seen any evidence for God, and anyway, Mr Symons, my biology teacher, says there is no God, and we are here because of evolution."

Uncle Matt smiled. "You know, there's a verse in the Bible about people who say there's no God. It says, 'The fool has said in his heart, "There is no God".' Seb," he continued, looking more serious, "you really should think for yourself and not just blindly follow others. You think you are right, but have you considered what it means if you are wrong? Those who don't trust Christ as their Saviour will be in hell for all eternity, so it's extremely serious."

They had been driving up a steep hill. Uncle Matt slowed as they crested the top. "And anyway, if you want some evidence for God, just look at that." Before them they could see a lush, green valley, illuminated by the golden sunlight and rising again in the distance to purple-tinged hills set against the backdrop of an impossibly blue sky.

"Do you really think that this view just randomly happened? That a 'big bang' and evolution could do this? To me it proclaims the existence of a Creator."

Seb grunted. Uncle Matt seemed so sure. Mum had mentioned

that he'd been to university, so he must be intelligent. And yet, despite his biology teacher's claims about no intelligent person believing in God, Uncle Matt did. It didn't make sense.

Chapter Four

On arriving back at the farm, Aunt Karen had shown Seb to his room – a bright, airy room at the front of the house, with cream patterned wallpaper and moss green curtains and bedding. Not really his taste, but it could be worse. He even had his own bathroom... his *en suite*, Aunt Karen had called it.

"You should get changed," she told him, handing him the neatly folded pile of clothes that Uncle Matt had bought earlier. "It's almost time to bring the cows in."

Seb sighed. These people were determined to make him work for his keep. What did he know about cows? He may have seen one on a school trip when he was about six. Now he was going to be expected to bring in a whole... *crowd... flock... swarm...*? What did you even call a number of cows?

Pulling a sweatshirt over his head, he inspected his appearance in the full length mirror in the corner of the room. He sighed. He didn't quite look like a farmer, but his friends would hardly recognise him now.

He dragged himself down the stairs and through the door into the living area. Aunt Karen was busy peeling potatoes, and Martha was colouring a picture at the kitchen table.

"Your wellies are at the back door, Seb," said Aunt Karen, smiling. "Lavinia is waiting for you outside."

Seb found the wellies and pulled them on. They felt strange after his trainers. He opened the back door. Lavinia was standing in a faded red sweatshirt, her green wellies back on her feet. She giggled when she saw Seb.

Seb glowered at her. "What's so funny now?" he snapped.

Lavinia bit her lip and ducked her head. "Sorry," she said softly, "but it's your wellies…"

"What's wrong with the wellies?" Seb growled. "Apart from the fact that they are the ugliest things I've ever seen."

Lavinia looked up. The amused twinkle hadn't quite disappeared. "You're supposed to tuck your jeans into your wellies," she said. "They're to keep your lower legs and feet clean. This way the only clothes that'll be clean will be your socks!"

Seb tried to stuff the trouser leg into the boot.

Lavinia shook her head. "Here, let me show you," she said, and proceeded to pull his boot off.

"Now, you need to grab your trouser leg, like this…" She caught the loose material at the front of his leg and folded it around to the back. "Then you put on your welly." Seb shoved his leg into the welly.

"Okay, I get the message," he mumbled, hastily fixing his other leg.

They set off across the yard, Jess leading the way. They walked between two sets of outbuildings and Lavinia pulled a gate across behind them. Then they reached a rough, grass-centred lane.

"The cows are in the far field today," Lavinia told him. "Which field they are in depends on how much grass there is. This one is the furthest from the yard. It's normally my job to bring the cows in every night and then I help Dad milk. In the mornings Joe comes to help milk. He's a farm hand who works for us part-time. It's too much work for one person on their own. And I'm glad I don't have to bring the cows in in the morning – Joe starts to milk at 5:30am."

"5:30!" exclaimed Seb, incredulously. That was the middle of the night in their house! If Dad was at home he slept until lunchtime.

"The cows have to be milked at the same times each day," said Lavinia. "It's better for them and they like routine. They'll be waiting at the gate when it's time to be milked."

The back lane led down a steep hill and then curved to the right where it followed a shallow stream. Halfway up the next hill, the lane ended with a gate to a field, where, true to Lavinia's word, a number of black and white cows were standing behind the gate, watching their approach.

"There they are," she said, smiling.

Seb stopped to catch his breath and regard the much-anticipated animals. They were so big! And they kept staring at him and blowing out puffs of breath through their large, wet noses. Lavinia went to swing open the gate. "Stand back," she called.

Suddenly the cows all began to make their way through the gate. Seb watched as they ambled past, large, milk-filled udders swinging as they walked. One particularly curious beast swung her large head around to look in his direction and he shrank back against the prickles and branches of the hedge. She was then nudged forward by an impatient one following behind and Seb sighed with relief. The cows were now coming with less frequency, and he could see Jess rounding up a few strays at the far side of the field, Lavinia hollering what seemed to Seb like a chant to encourage them. It sounded as if she was calling, "AH-mon, AH-mon, AH-mon!" Whatever it was, it appeared to be working as the last remaining cows lumbered towards her.

Suddenly he felt a damp *whuff* right in his ear, immediately followed by a shove in his side. He lost his balance and sprawled in the dirt. Standing over him was a large, mostly black cow with a small white patch on her forehead. Seb scrambled, but couldn't gain his footing. "LAVINIA!" he screamed. The beast took another step towards him, lowered her head once more. Her large eyes were dark and glazed. Seb's hand landed in something warm, soft and extremely smelly. It slid through the slimy mess and he fell backwards again. The cow's head lowered and Seb closed his eyes to brace himself for certain death. He felt the warm breath, smelled its unique gassy odour... and suddenly a wet sandpaper tongue scratched across his cheek.

"Mirabelle!" Lavinia's voice, accompanied by booted footsteps, came closer. "Mirabelle! What do you think you're doing?"

The large head moved upwards at the sound of her voice and Seb took the opportunity to make good his escape. He was trembling from his head right down to his toes encased in the now filthy wellies. Lavinia put a hand on either side of the large cow's face and rubbed the shiny black cheeks. "Naughty girl," she scolded softly. "You shouldn't scare our visitor. He's never met a cow before and that was a terrible first impression you gave him. Hm-hmm, bad girl," she cooed. She slapped her lightly on the shoulder and the large, black beast turned around and moved off, pausing once to look back at Seb with dark, menacing eyes. Seb shuddered. She seemed to be saying, "Just wait, I'll get you next time."

Lavinia turned to Seb. "Are you all right?" she asked, biting her lip.

Seb shrugged. "Yeah!" He lifted his hand to rub his face, then noticed the greeny-brown muck on his hand. He kicked the gatepost in anger and rubbed his hand on his jeans.

"I'm sorry about that," Lavinia said. "Most cows have a healthy respect for humans and won't come too close, but that Mirabelle... I don't know why, but she seems to think she's better than the rest of the cows! She was just being friendly; she's a big softie!"

Seb grunted. His cousin hadn't seen the murderous look Mirabelle had given him when he was lying on the ground.

Jess drove the remaining three cows past where they were standing and on down the lane towards the yard. Lavinia followed, with Seb dragging his heels a few steps behind.

Lavinia appeared to have a twitch around her mouth, and every so often her shoulders shook. Finally, she could contain herself no longer and burst out laughing.

"I'm so…so…sorry!" she giggled. "The look on your face, and Mirabelle trying to lick you to death. And the cow dung everywhere…" She stopped and bent over, trying to control the laughter which spilled over and rang across the green hills. She fished for a tissue and wiped her eyes. "If you could have seen yourself!"

Seb glared at her and stomped off in a rage. He *hated* this place. He hated being out of his comfort zone, at home it might not have been pleasant, but at least everything was predictable and he could escape.

By now, the cows had long since gone. He could see them in the distance, entering one of the sheds.

Seb broke into a jog. He wanted to put as much distance as possible between him and his obnoxious cousin. He could feel the stones of the lane beneath the soles of his wellies and occasionally almost lost his footing on the slippery deposits left behind by the black and white monsters.

"Seb! SEB! Wait! I'm sorry!" he heard Lavinia call behind him, but he increased his speed, ignoring the sharp pain in his side. He wasn't used to running so fast and in such unsuitable footwear, but hurt and anger drove him on.

Reaching the yard, he climbed the gate which was blocking his way and tumbled down the other side. Where could he go now? Lavinia was rounding the bend in the lane and would soon catch up. He couldn't go into the house: Aunt Karen and Martha were in the kitchen and they'd want to know why he was so dishevelled and dirty. He spotted the truck parked in the yard, beside the shed where the sawdust was kept, and he tried the driver's door – it was open. Sliding in, he hunkered in the footwell. He heard Lavinia swing herself over the gate and land with a booted thud on the ground. He held his breath, and finally heard the milking parlour door slide back. Gingerly, he lifted his head and peered out of the window. Lavinia slipped through the door and slid it back into place. Waiting a few more seconds, Seb unfolded himself and climbed onto the seat.

The sight of the interior momentarily took his mind off his humiliating experience, and even the strong, obnoxious smell from his hands, clothes and boots seemed to recede as he ran his hands over the leather steering wheel. He wondered how it would feel to drive this amazing vehicle. He found the lever to adjust his seat and slid it forward until his foot touched the accelerator. He slipped on the seat belt and sat for a moment, pressing the clutch and changing gears, pretending to steer.

Suddenly, he noticed the keys in the ignition. He wondered if anyone would hear him if he turned it on. He was far enough from the house, and there was a loud humming noise coming from the milking parlour. He pressed the clutch and turned the key. The big machine roared to life. Seb's heart started to pound. This was much better than the Ford Fiesta belonging to his friend Tyler's mum, which they used to drive around the carpark of the retail park next to his house.

Slipping the big truck into gear, he released the handbrake, then pressed the accelerator and shot off. Steering down the lane, he glanced in the wing mirror to see if anyone had noticed. No one appeared. He felt a pricking of his conscience. He would only drive to the bottom of the lane and back. No one would ever know. Before he knew it, he had reached the end of the lane. He braked hard; momentarily hesitated. *Already?* He shrugged, then turned left onto the road, and mashed the accelerator. The truck responded, and Seb changed gears. The road was straight and there were no other cars. Seb laughed. This was the life. *Finally*, he thought, *a bit of fun!* Seb looked at the speedometer – 50…55…60. Suddenly, the road veered to the left and Seb braked sharply.

He could feel the back end swing wide and he steered out to correct it, but it was too late. As he frantically braked, the truck spun out of control. The steep bank loomed close and Seb closed his eyes and gripped the wheel. Seb was flung against the door as the truck tipped dangerously to one side and rolled onto its roof, with an almighty crash and huge bang. Seb found himself dangling upside down by his seatbelt. The cab was hazy and Seb was numb with shock. He fumbled for the seatbelt release and dropped in a crumpled heap.

Just then, there was a banging at the window and a grizzled old face, topped with a tweed cap, peered into the cab.

"Matt! Matt, are you..." The old man blinked. He tried the door, but it was jammed shut. Rushing round to the other side, he pulled open the door and peered in. "Who in the name o' goodness are you, and what are you doin' with Matt's vehicle?"

"I'm Seb," answered Seb. He glanced at the steering wheel, noticing the crack in the plastic covering with a deflated white airbag hanging from it.

The old man lifted his cap and scratched his head. "Just you stay there, young man," he said, pulling a big, old mobile phone from his pocket. "I'm phonin' Matt, and then I'm phonin' the police. Are you hurt? I'll ask for the ambulance too."

The words *Matt* and *police* jolted Seb upright. "Oh no, please, mister, please don't phone the police," he pled. But the old man had closed the door and was holding the phone to his ear, a grim look on his wizened old face.

Seb stood beside Uncle Matt, head bowed. The pickup truck was resting on its roof, badly dented, with glass strewn across the road. Uncle Matt had talked his neighbour out of phoning the police. He had appeared in two minutes, still dressed in a green waterproof milking apron. After determining that Seb was unhurt, Matt had phoned a neighbour with a recovery vehicle. While they were waiting, the three stood and looked at the damage.

"A write-off, I'd say," the old man spoke, rubbing his grey stubble.

"Looks like it, Tommy," Matt replied, nodding solemnly.

"It's only in the mercy of God you weren't killed," Tommy addressed Seb, shaking his head.

Seb remained silent.

A yellow and red lorry appeared around the bend and pulled in.

"My word, Matt!" the lanky driver exclaimed as he got out. "You've done a brave bit of damage!" He squinted his eyes. "Or *was* it you?" he asked, noticing that Matt was still wearing his milking apron, and there were too many vehicles around for the number of adults.

"Not quite," Matt said, after a pause. "But we'd better get it off the road before anyone else has an accident."

The beat up truck was loaded onto the lorry and Larry headed down the road. It looked even worse right side up. Seb couldn't quite believe he was unhurt.

"I'll be down later, Tommy. Thanks for all your help." Matt waved at Tommy and put an arm around Seb's shoulders to direct him to the little red car Seb had seen in the yard earlier.

Seb climbed in and looked at the ground. So far Uncle Matt had been calm, but he knew it wouldn't last. He braced himself for the storm.

Chapter Five

Dinner was a silent affair that evening. Aunt Karen attempted to make conversation, but the monosyllabic answers from the other occupants made it difficult. Uncle Matt seemed preoccupied and Seb imagined he was likely thinking of what he would say to Seb's mum when he phoned her to arrange to send him back home first thing tomorrow morning. Lavinia had barely looked at him since they arrived back in the yard; the one look of loathing and disgust she cast at him told Seb all he needed to know about her reaction to his escapade. Even Martha was aware something was wrong, sitting wide-eyed, poking at her peas with her fork.

Seb couldn't wait until dinner was over and he could escape back to his room. He didn't want to be around this family, feeling their judgmental glances and unspoken disapproval. He wasn't hungry anyway.

Finally dinner was over. Seb made a beeline for the door.

"Seb!" Uncle Matt called.

Seb froze. This was it. Now he was going to get what he'd been expecting ever since Uncle Matt saw his bashed up truck.

"Seb, come back here!"

He braced himself for the inevitable and slowly turned round.

"We all help with clearing the table here," Uncle Matt told him.

"But that's a *girl's* job!" Seb whined.

Lavinia's mouth dropped open, and she slammed the pile of plates she was holding back on to the table.

"Well, that's rich!" she exclaimed. "A *girl's* job, is it? And what do you consider milking cows, cleaning out calf houses, helping with silaging and spreading slurry are? And what exactly do men do in your world, apart from crashing expensive vehicles which they've *stolen!* You are *scum* and I HATE you! I wish you would go back to Belfast where you belong and stop ruining everything for us, you…"

"Lavinia!" Uncle Matt scolded. "That's enough! Lift those plates to the sink and not another word."

Seb clenched his fists and tried to suppress the urge to hit his cousin. This was the worst day of his entire life. He turned and ran through the living area, yanking open the door and slamming it again behind him. He took the stairs two at a time and ran around the landing to his room. He pulled his rucksack out from under the bed and began to stuff all his belongings into it. He wouldn't take his new 'farmer' clothes. He wouldn't need those back in Belfast.

"Seb?" came Uncle Matt's voice, accompanied by a light rap at the door. "Can I come in?"

Seb froze. He didn't want to see anyone. He just wanted to go home.

The door was pushed open a little and Uncle Matt's head appeared. He frowned. "What are you doing?" he asked.

"Packing," muttered Seb.

"Why?" asked Uncle Matt, coming into the room and sitting in the green chair beside the window.

Seb shrugged. "Am I not going home?" he asked, defiantly lifting his chin.

Uncle Matt leaned back in the chair and rested his ankle on his other knee. "Why would you think that?"

Seb looked away. He didn't speak.

"Is it because you thought I'd be so angry I'd send you away?"

Seb shrugged again.

"The way your dad did when you set the living room on fire?"

Seb's head drooped and he began to pick at his nails.

"Seb, sit down a minute. I want to tell you something."

Seb dropped himself onto the bed and began to poke at the green blanket. He figured he knew what was coming.

"Seb, I want to tell you a story."

Seb glanced up. He'd expected a telling off at the very least. He certainly didn't expect a story! Uncle Matt didn't look angry either. He seemed calm, but looked sad. And there was even something like pity in his eyes. Pity for Seb. He dropped his gaze back to the blanket. He was Seb! He was tough! He didn't need pity!

"I grew up in a wonderful home," Uncle Matt began. "I had two parents who loved each other and loved me and all my younger brothers and sisters very much. They taught us right from wrong, and took us to church regularly. And until I was around 13 I was happy. By then, I'd changed schools and met other kids who seemed to have much more fun than I did. I started to feel that my life was boring and I wanted to have some fun. I started to hang around with these boys. I got into all sorts of things – I smoked, I drank, I even messed about with drugs."

Seb's head shot up, his eyes wide. "You?!" he exclaimed.

Uncle Matt gave a sad smile. "Yes, I'm afraid so," he said. "I'm not at all proud of those days. In fact, I'm totally ashamed of the person I was then, and that wasn't the worst of it. One night we had been hanging around drinking and smoking weed. One of the boys, Darren was his name, suggested taking his brother's car for a drive. None of us were old enough to drive or in any fit state to be driving even if we had been. There were seven of us and it was only a small car, so no one was wearing a seatbelt. I'll not go into the details, but Darren was driving way too fast, on roads he really didn't know, having drunk numerous cans of beer. It was never going to end well. We hit a tree and most of those boys were killed. One ended up brain damaged and paralysed for life. I was the only one who walked away from that accident."

Uncle Matt paused, rummaging in his pockets. Seb glanced up, astounded to see the big, tough man with tears in his eyes.

"I often think about those boys," he went on. "I had been brought up differently. I knew that there is a heaven and there is a hell, and the only way I'd ever be in heaven is if I trusted in God's Son, the Lord Jesus Christ, Who was punished for our sins, but I had rejected His love. If I had been killed in that accident, I'd have been in hell right now, and would have been there forever. God is gracious. It wasn't long before I accepted Christ as my Saviour."

Seb said nothing. It didn't make much sense to him, but it was obviously very real to Uncle Matt.

"That's why I was so worried when Tommy phoned me to say you had crashed the truck. Because I know what can happen, and you aren't saved... you aren't ready to die. I'm so thankful you weren't hurt."

Seb dug his nail into the blanket. "But, Uncle Matt, aren't you mad at me?" he asked in a small voice.

"I can't say I'm happy about losing my truck, Seb," he admitted. "It cost me a lot of hard-earned money, and I know the insurance won't cover it as the keys were left in it, so I won't be able to replace it."

Seb winced. He hadn't thought of that. In fact, he hadn't really thought at all before he gave in to temptation. And now Uncle Matt's truck was gone forever, Lavinia was mad at him, and he had just given one more reason for his mum to cry and his dad to get mad at him. He felt small and wicked.

"I'm sorry," he said, almost under his breath.

Uncle Matt got up and knelt on the floor in front of him. He took him by the shoulders. "Look at me, Seb," he said.

Seb raised his eyes. Uncle Matt didn't look angry. In fact, he was even smiling.

"I forgive you," he said.

Seb blinked, astonished. "Why?" he asked.

"Seb, you remember I said earlier that I had rejected God's love?"

Seb nodded. It felt very strange to hear someone speak of God as if He was actually real. But he wasn't going to argue with Uncle Matt tonight, not when he was being so nice to Seb.

"Well," Uncle Matt continued, "when I was brought to my senses and trusted God's Son, I realised that all my sins had been forgiven because of His death for me. And when I have been forgiven so much, God expects me to forgive others, no matter how difficult that may be."

Seb pondered Uncle Matt's words. He couldn't help compare what he'd just said with what he knew his dad's reaction would have been. He shuddered at the thought. What made the difference? Surely it wasn't *religion*?

"The only other thing, Seb, and I want you to understand that I'm not doing this out of spite, or going back on my word, but there is something you need to learn. When God forgave me He didn't just hide my sins somewhere and say, 'Ah, we'll just not worry about them anymore.' I had sinned against Him and my sins needed to be punished, but, as I said, God punished His Son in my place. Sin needs to be punished, and even when you've been forgiven, sin still has consequences. I'm not going to send you away. I really don't feel that would be best for you, but I've discussed this with Karen and we are in agreement. For the remainder of your time here we are going to confiscate your smartphone."

Seb sat bolt upright. His phone! "Uncle Matt," he pleaded. "Please don't take away my phone! I'll never survive without it."

Uncle Matt shook his head sadly. "Sorry, Seb, but we wanted the punishment to fit the crime. What you did was wrong, and you know it. Now, hand it over."

Seb reached into his pocket. His one link with the outside world... how would he ever manage now? Slowly, he placed the phone in Matt's outstretched hand.

"Thanks, Seb," he said, turning it off and slipping it into his jeans' pocket. He patted him on the shoulder and stood up. "Now, get an early night and sleep well. We've lots to do tomorrow."

Uncle Matt walked towards the door, then paused. "One last thing, Seb," he said, turning around. "Your Aunt Karen and I, we love you. Don't forget that."

He softly left the room and closed the door behind him.

Chapter Six

Seb woke feeling refreshed, despite having lain awake for a long time. He wasn't used to the silence and the darkness of the country, and the chiming of the grandfather clock had seemed to mock his sleeplessness, marking off every fifteen minutes of the interminably long night. The day's events had continued to roll around in his head and he felt he would never be able to sleep.

But morning had arrived. Seb looked at the fancy little bedside clock – 7:30am. He stretched and yawned. If he was at home he would have rolled over and gone back to sleep, but he figured that here he was likely the last one to get up. Milking would be nearly over by now. He crossed the room to the window and pulled back the heavy curtains. It looked like it had rained during the night, but today was a beautiful summer's day. His window overlooked the well-tended garden. Beyond the neat hedge lay a field which sloped down to the road. He followed the line of the road to the left and spotted a small farmhouse and red outbuildings in the distance between two hills. It was the only house he could see – any view to the right was obscured by the tall fir trees lining the lane. He really was miles from civilisation here!

Quickly dressing in some of the clothes Uncle Matt had bought for him – was it only yesterday? – he padded down the stairs in his socks. A delicious smell wafted up to greet him.

Aunt Karen was standing at the Aga, a pale blue apron wrapped around her tiny waist, frying bacon and eggs. She turned when she heard Seb come in.

"Good morning, Seb," she said, smiling. "How did you sleep?"

"Morning," Seb grunted. "It took me awhile. It's far too quiet here."

Aunt Karen chuckled. "I'm sure you'll get used to it," she said. "I'd likely struggle to sleep with all the noises in the city. Are you hungry?"

Seb's stomach growled.

"Well, that answers my question! It won't be long before Matt and Lavinia are in. And Joe..." she broke off. "Did Matt or Lavinia tell you about Joe, our farm labourer?"

Seb nodded.

"Good. Well, Joe usually has breakfast with us too. I just need to get Martha up and dressed. Would you mind lifting the orange juice out of the fridge?"

Seb walked across to the big fridge-freezer and opened the door. It was crammed full with all sorts of food – yoghurts, packages of meat, cooked ham, fresh vegetables, cheese, plastic tubs of every size and description. The fridge at home had usually more cans of beer than food. He found the orange juice in the door and brought it over to the table.

"Oh, sorry, Seb," Aunt Karen went on. "I should have asked you to bring the tomato sauce as well – these farmers can't have their Ulster fry without some red sauce! Some like brown sauce, but it has to be red sauce in this house!"

Aunt Karen kept him busy while she finished cooking the food. Stacking it on a large platter she slipped it into the bottom oven of the Aga to keep warm while she went to get Martha.

Seb pulled out a chair and sat at the table. Aunt Karen hadn't mentioned the truck incident at all. In fact, she'd almost acted like it had never happened. He didn't suppose he'd get away so lightly with Lavinia. And to have to be introduced to Joe as 'the boy who stole and crashed the pickup truck on his first day here' made him cringe.

Another thought entered his mind which made him shudder. Was it possible that Uncle Matt could have changed his mind about forgiving him? After all, this was the first day he would have to do all his farm work without the truck.

The noise of the back door opening shook him from his reverie. This was it. They were here.

Lavinia was the first to enter the farmhouse kitchen, with her dad close behind. She glanced at Seb, then looked away.

"Morning, Seb," Uncle Matt said pleasantly. Seb breathed a sigh of relief. Lavinia didn't appear to be speaking to him, but at least Uncle Matt hadn't turned angry overnight.

"Morning," Seb replied, lifting the nearest fork and turning it between his fingers.

"Lavinia," called Matt.

"Yes, Dad?" she asked, hesitatingly.

"Aren't you going to speak to Seb?"

She sighed. "Good morning, Seb!" she said, brightly. Too brightly. Her dark eyes flashed with barely-restrained animosity.

"Morning," Seb muttered.

The door opened again and a tall, young man came in. He had dark, exceedingly curly hair, and blue eyes set in a face with a wide, pleasant grin.

"So this is Seb." He pulled out the chair opposite Seb and sat down, crossing his tanned, brawny arms over his green shirt. "From Belfast, are you?"

Seb nodded.

"I've folks who live in Belfast. Used to love going to visit when I was your age. So much going on."

Finally. Someone else who appreciated civilisation!

Aunt Karen and Martha came into the room at that point. "Great, you're all here," she said. "Take your seats and I'll get breakfast served up."

Seb thoroughly enjoyed his breakfast – fried eggs, sausages, bacon, mushrooms, baked beans, soda bread, and something they called *fadge*, which Aunt Karen explained was potato bread.

After they finished, Uncle Matt reached for his Bible. Seb ducked his head and rolled his eyes. He was grateful Uncle Matt had forgiven him, whatever the reason he gave, but Seb still felt a sense of revulsion at the sight of the big, black book. He had almost forgotten that these people were deceived so badly; they were so pleasant and seemed so normal. He wasn't going to make a fuss though, not after his less than wonderful actions yesterday.

"Today we're reading in Psalm number 19," Uncle Matt said, flicking through the thin pages. He paused. "This is one of my favourites.

" 'The heavens declare the glory of God; and the firmament shows His handiwork. Day unto day utters speech, and night unto night reveals knowledge. There is no speech nor language where their voice is not heard. Their line has gone out through all the earth, and their words to the end of the world. In them He has set a tabernacle for the sun, which is like a bridegroom coming out of his chamber, and rejoices like a strong man to run its race. Its rising is from one end of heaven, and its circuit to the other end; and there is nothing hidden from its heat...' "

Seb found it difficult to understand what it all meant, but he was intrigued. It was almost a bit like poetry, not at all how he expected the Bible to sound. He had never read the Bible, in fact, he wasn't sure if there was even one in his house. He didn't think there was, unless his mum had one hidden away somewhere.

Uncle Matt finished reading and looked around the table. "Now," he said, smiling, "I'm sure there are questions!"

"Me first, Daddy," said Martha.

"Okay, go ahead, princess."

"Why does it talk about a furry mint?"

"Furry mint?" asked Matt, frowning.

"Yes, Daddy," Martha said. "It says the furry mint shows God's handy work."

Aunt Karen put her hand to her mouth, but her eyes danced.

"Ah! It's 'firmament'," corrected Matt, smiling. " 'The firmament shows God's handiwork.' Another translation calls it 'the sky above'. And 'handiwork' just means 'the work of His hands.' This psalm is talking about how creation shows God's glory – so even those who have never heard God's name know there must have been a Creator. All they need to do is look up! There are billions and billions of stars, all proclaiming God's glory."

Seb snorted.

"You don't agree, Seb," Uncle Matt said. It was more of a statement than a question.

Seb shook his head. "The universe began with the Big Bang," he said. "Sure everyone knows that. That's what all the scientists say."

"Really?" Uncle Matt asked. "You'd need to ask them all to be sure! There are a number who don't believe it, you know! I've a question for you, Seb. How do you think this Big Bang started?"

Seb shrugged. "There was something that exploded."

"But how was the 'something' there in the first place? And what made it explode?"

Seb scratched his head. He couldn't remember what Miss Carruthers had said when they studied it in physics.

"You know the galaxies stretch further than we can even imagine? Yet you're telling me that the material to form all these galaxies was contained in a small particle. And how did the whole thing end up so ordered?"

Uncle Matt pushed his plate aside and set his Bible on the table before continuing.

"Imagine a rocket being sent into space. The people on board couldn't live in space without things like air, water and food, so everything they need for survival must be on that rocket."

Seb glanced around the table. Everyone was engrossed in what Uncle Matt was saying; even little Martha was sitting wide-eyed.

"Now," he continued, "think about this! We are on earth, a planet which is hurtling through space, but everything we need for survival is in place. Do you know why that is?"

"Beats me, Matt," shrugged Joe, leaning back in his chair and folding his arms.

"The rocket was designed to preserve life, and so is this world! Did you know that we are exactly the right distance from the sun to sustain life? Think about the effect on water if we weren't. If earth was a little closer to the sun, we would only have steam, a little further away and it would all be ice."

"Goodness!" exclaimed Joe. "I never thought of that!"

Seb bit his lip. He hadn't thought of that either. But that didn't mean to say the Big Bang didn't happen, did it? Surely it could have happened by chance?

"Someone once said that the chance of a big bang producing a universe such as ours is equivalent to a hurricane blowing through a scrapyard and assembling a fully functional aeroplane! One thing I'm sure of, Seb, and that is that accepting the evidence for a Creator is much easier than believing in a random happening."

Aunt Karen nodded. " 'In the beginning God created the heavens and the earth,' " she quoted. "Did you know, Seb, that the accepted view of scientists nowadays is that the universe had a definite point of beginning? This wasn't always the case. Many scientists thought that the universe always existed and to say that it actually had a point where it began looked too much like creation to them so they wouldn't accept it! They may not have come to accept a Creator, but they've been forced to accept a beginning."

Seb grunted. It all sounded so plausible and made a lot of sense.

Yet what did these people really know? They were biased. And what about evolution? He'd need more than a few facts if he was to change his mind.

Chapter Seven

Seb followed Uncle Matt and Lavinia across the yard towards the whitewashed farmhouse. The door lay open and Matt ducked his head to enter the low doorway. He rapped twice on the internal door, before turning the wooden doorknob and entering a dark kitchen, dominated by a brown stove. A table covered with a red-patterned oilcloth sat below the window, a bright spot of colour in a room dominated by too much brown. An old man sat reading in the rocking chair to one side of the stove, and, as he looked up, Seb recognised the grizzled face as the same one that had appeared through the open door of the beat up truck yesterday.

"Well, Matt!" he exclaimed, the wrinkles on his face multiplying as he broke into a sparsely-toothed grin. "How's things the day?"

"Doing grand, Tommy," Matt replied, lowering himself onto a kitchen chair and resting an elbow on the table. Lavinia plopped down on the rough brown couch, and Seb sat on the other end, wishing he was invisible.

The old man's eyes peered out from under furry grey brows.

"Lavinia, dear!" he said. "Good to see you. You got your holidays, have you?"

Lavinia nodded. "Thank goodness!" she exclaimed.

"And Seb."

Seb breathed sharply in. This was the point he was dreading.

"Hope you'd no after e-ffects from your mishap yesterday."

Seb glanced up to see genuine concern in the pale, watery eyes.

"I'm fine," he muttered. "Thanks."

The door burst open and a short, round lady bustled in.

"Oh, oh, oh!" she panted, pulling the blue headscarf from her head and trying in vain to flatten down the grey bush that sprouted in all directions from her head. "I saw the car comin' in and I said tae mesel', says I, that there's Matt comin', and I need tae get the kettle on and make some tae for ye. Thon dog is a pain in the backside. He takes off and he'll no come when ye shout!"

Seb watched in amazement as the whirlwind dashed out again, returning half a minute later minus her dark green coat, with her feet now encased in navy slippers.

She paused when she spotted Seb.

"So you're Karen's nephew?" she asked, peering at him. "I don't see any likeness. You're awful *fair*," she added, dubiously. "Though ye don't seem that wile tall. Karen's a wee slip o' a thing, too, I s'pose. Is it your mother that's Karen's sister?"

Seb nodded.

"And is she older or younger?"

Seb shrugged. He didn't actually know. The McRoss family hadn't exactly been a popular topic of conversation during his childhood.

"Karen's younger, by about a year," Uncle Matt said. "And I think Seb has some family traits, all right! Sure our Martha's fair."

The woman spun round to face Uncle Matt. "I s'pose you're right," she said. "I always wondered where Martha got her colourin'. You two are so dark, and Lavinia is the spit o' you!"

She suddenly remembered Lavinia was in the room as well. "Well, dear, good tae see ye. Ye don't come enough, ye know. Us oul pair likes young company. Ye should come more often, give us a share o' your chat! How's school going? Oh, that's right - it's the holidays, isn't it? And how's that Jess-dog o' yours doin'? Any word o' those pups yet? I think we should get rid o' thon Rex nuisance out there. He's nothin' but bother. Couldn't work tae save his life."

She moved over to the stove and lifted a kettle, disappearing into a little room through the door to the left of the stove. She continued to chatter, extolling the virtues of Matt's 'Jess-dog' and the misdemeanours of Rex, while she set the kettle on the stove and disappeared into the pantry again.

Seb leaned over to Lavinia. "Who is she?" he whispered.

"Madge," she whispered back. "Tommy's sister. She *never* stops talking."

"Really?" said Seb, his eyes wide. "I hadn't noticed!"

Lavinia stifled a giggle behind her hand.

Madge reappeared, her large, rough hands holding five mugs, which she plopped on the table.

"Did ye hear Bobby Davison down by The Burnside got four head o' cattle stolen last night? The boys came in the middle o' the night and he never heard a thing. But he is wile deaf, all the same. He wouldn't hear ye if ye yelled in his ear."

"And I'm sure you tried it, Madge," Tommy muttered, raising an eyebrow at Lavinia and Seb, a twinkle in his blue eyes.

"Hey, what, what? What'd ye just say, Tommy? I hope ye weren't pokin' fun at me, for that's no on, ye know! Where was I? Oh aye, Bobby Davison, being deaf as a post. Sure I was down at McGrath's the other day and I saw Bobby buyin' washing powder. Zap, it was. Don't know why the man buys Zap. Sure it smells rotten and it's as dear as poison. Poor Sadie, having tae wash wi' *thon*! I prefer Breeze mesel'. Nothin' like Breeze for bringin' the white up good again. And then there's these young ones that don't use starch anymore! Can ye imagine? I hope Karen uses starch, Matt..."

"Any word o' the tae, Madge?" Tommy broke in. "That kettle's startin' to boil."

Madge threw her hands in the air and rushed back to the stove. "So it is, Tommy. I never even heard that! I don't think your hearin' is as bad as ye make it out tae be sometimes. No as bad as Bobby's anyway. I don't know why he doesn't get one o' thon hearin' aids. I think the health service even pays for them. Now, I think that's us. Come on, weans, sit over. I've some o' thon big cream buns you like, Matt, and I made up a big batch o' gypsy creams the other day. And the minurl man was here yesterday, Lavinia, so I've a new bottle o' Iron Brew. I've poured ye some in thon cream mug. What'd you like, Seb? The same? It's quare stuff, though I shouldn't be drinking it. I'm s'posed tae be diabetic, ye know. But, boys, it's wile hard tae keep off the sugary stuff..."

"Uncle Matt," asked Seb on the way back to Cherryhill Farm, "what is a 'minurl man'?"

Matt threw back his head and laughed. "Oh, Seb," he said. "We speak another language in this part of the world, don't we? Were you able to understand Madge at all?"

"A bit," Seb replied, "but she made my head spin."

Uncle Matt clutched the steering wheel. His deep laughter bounced around the small car. "She makes mine spin too, Seb, and I can understand her perfectly! But she's a good soul, you know. So kind and would do anything for anybody. But back to your question. A 'minurl man', as she talks about, is a man who comes around in a wee lorry and delivers fizzy drinks, or 'mineral' as some old folks call it, around the country. Madge is likely his best customer!"

"That orange fizzy stuff she gave us was good," remarked Seb.

Matt nodded. "It's similar to the Irn Bru in Scotland. I must have drunk gallons of the stuff when I was at university there. The Northern Ireland replica is just as good, although don't tell the Scottish people that!"

"And those biscuits joined together with chocolate," Seb continued. "I've never heard of them before."

"Gypsy creams," Lavinia piped up from the back. "They're Dad's favourite. She spoils him!"

"They're good," agreed Matt. "Maybe you should learn to make them, Vinnie."

Lavinia snorted. "I'd rather be out milking cows."

"But you'll maybe get married someday," her dad replied. "And what if that Caleb boy wants gypsy creams?"

"DAD!" exclaimed Lavinia, as they arrived back at Cherryhill. "What makes you think I'm going to marry Caleb? And, anyway," she continued, as she opened the car door and hopped out, "there's no reason why boys shouldn't bake gypsy creams."

Matt chuckled and winked at Seb. "She's easy wound up, is our Vinnie!"

The next morning, Seb followed Uncle Matt across the yard. He had appeared from the office when he heard Seb coming down the stairs.

"Joe and Vinnie are milking," he'd told him. "I need your help."

Seb didn't know what he had in mind until they stopped beside a bright blue tractor. Up close, it was huge! Seb felt dwarfed beside the large wheel. Uncle Matt reached up and swung open the door. "Climb in," he said.

Seb looked at him, then back at the tractor. Uncle Matt must need the tractor for the work he'd planned. He reached up, grasped the handle beside the door and swung himself onto the step and clambered into the cab. It seemed very far above the ground.

"Sit down," called Uncle Matt.

"Where?" asked Seb.

"On the driver's seat!"

Seb stared at Uncle Matt. He had to be joking! Did he mean for him to drive? Surely not!

Matt climbed up after him, reached out to close the door and propped himself on the small seat at one side.

"There's a lever under the seat to adjust it."

"Are you wanting me to drive?" asked Seb.

"That's the plan," replied Matt. "If you're going to stay here all summer, you need to know how to drive a tractor, and," he added, with a slight smile, "I'd rather teach you than you taking it into your head yourself."

Seb winced.

Uncle Matt patted his shoulder. "Now, come on, let's get that seat at the right distance for you."

Seb followed his uncle's instructions and they soon began to move across the yard. Uncle Matt directed him down the back lane and they rocked along the rough stones. It felt a lot different from the other vehicles he'd ever driven, but it started to feel natural and Seb enjoyed being in control of the powerful tractor. When they reached the field where the cows had been grazing, Seb slowed and turned in the open gateway. Uncle Matt directed Seb to the edge of the field, where a long white strip of plastic which ran across the field met the hedge. It seemed to be suspended a few feet off the ground on small white posts. It didn't look very sturdy.

"That's an electric fence," Uncle Matt answered Seb's unspoken query. "The cows know not to touch it, or they'll get a shock. Don't let Joe trick you into touching it," he added, grinning. "That'd be like a trick he'd play on someone unsuspecting!"

Uncle Matt backed out of the cab and motioned Seb to follow. He stood up and started to climb down the steps.

"Backwards," called Matt. Seb turned around and reversed out of the cab. He was glad the cows were being milked.

"We need to change the fence," Matt said, striding across to the small box joined to the fence and flipping a switch. "This turns off the power, so it's safe to touch," he explained.

Together they moved the fence a few feet farther down the field to give the cows another strip of fresh grass.

As they finished, Seb looked around to see the cows returning to the field. His heart was in his throat. He was not looking forward to being in close proximity to the large, nosy animals again. The large beasts ambled towards the lush green grass. Seb backed towards the hedge. One lifted her head and looked in Seb's direction. She seemed to sniff the air and Seb couldn't help but imagine that, like the giant in the story of the small boy and the beanstalk, she was thinking *fee fi fo fum, I smell the blood...*

"Seb?" Uncle Matt called. "What's wrong?" He walked through the long grass to where Seb was standing.

Seb looked at Matt and nodded towards the animal. "She doesn't like me."

"Mirabelle? Gentle giant!" Matt grinned. "Here she comes."

Sure enough, the black beast was heading their way. Seb clenched his fists. He would not run this time.

Mirabelle made her way to Uncle Matt and nudged his arm. He reached up and scratched her shoulder. With a gentle *whuff* in Matt's ear she stepped closer. He laughed and pushed her away. "That's not polite!" he told her.

He turned to Seb. "Come here," he said. "Let's introduce you properly."

Seb's heart was beating like crazy and he was shaking like a leaf, but he didn't want Uncle Matt to know. He took a step forward. Mirabelle watched him, her large, moist eyes framed by long, dark eyelashes. Strangely, she didn't look scary now, only curious. Her large ears twitched and he could see the individual hairs silhouetted against the bright sunlight.

Slowly, Seb made his way to the object of his fear and reached out a shaky hand. She touched his outstretched hand with her wet, slimy nose and let out another *whuff*. Taking a step closer, he touched her smooth, silky, black cheek. She shook her head around and moved closer to Seb. He felt like running, but stood his ground. His hand touched her shoulder and he gave it a scratch, as he had seen Uncle Matt do. Mirabelle leaned towards him. Seb froze. WHUFF! Right in his ear! Funny, last time it was scary. This time it just tickled. He laughed and looked up at her. She seemed to be laughing back!

Matt chuckled. "There you go, Seb, friends for life, I'd say! Come on, let's go for breakfast. We'll come out again afterwards. Your agricultural machine handling lesson isn't over yet."

Before Karen called them in for lunch, Uncle Matt had taught Seb to hitch a trailer to the tractor. He'd also begun to teach him how to manoeuvre corners and tight openings.

"Seb," he said, as they walked across the yard to the house. "You've done well this morning. You've worked hard, you faced your fear of cows, and you have a real ability handling the tractor and trailer. I'm proud of you!" He reached across and patted him on the back.

Seb looked at the ground and bit his lip. He didn't know what to say. Praise wasn't something he was used to. In fact, he couldn't remember a time his father had ever told him he was proud of him. He'd enjoyed learning new things and the sense of achievement gave him a buzz he'd never known before. And then to be the object of Uncle Matt's praise... Maybe this summer would work out okay after all.

Chapter Eight

"You want what?" The big-bellied salesman looked incredulously at Uncle Matt. "What happened to that L200 I sold you in March?"

Seb swallowed and ducked his head.

Matt kicked at the tyre of the nearest vehicle, a grey Land Rover Defender. "One of those things, Barry," he replied vaguely.

The man leaned forward, the smell of his over-applied Brut aftershave strong in the afternoon heat. "Did you go and sell it? Or did something happen to it?"

Matt shrugged. "I just need something to keep me going, not too expensive…"

Barry stood back and regarded Matt through narrowed eyes. Seeming to realise that further questioning would yield no answers, he pointed down the yard. "Well, I've the very thing over here," he said. "Follow me."

Matt, Seb and Lavinia strolled behind him as he sauntered down the yard. He seemed to need to use his momentum to propel himself forward, and rocked from side to side with each step he took. The large black shirt was untucked, and the top few buttons open to reveal a carpet of black hair, crowned with a thick gold chain around his neck.

Stopping beside a jeep, he opened the driver's door. "What about this, Matt?" he asked. "It's 10 years old, has a fair number of miles, but isn't giving any bother. Good price."

Matt circled the red jeep, inspecting the bodywork and the wheels. He took a look inside, then popped the bonnet open and began to scrutinise the inner workings. Lavinia had wandered across the yard and was looking at a large, blue Ford pickup truck. Its plates just read 'RANGER' and it looked like new. Seb joined her.

"This is more like what Dad would like," she said. "He's never been a big fan of jeeps. But it's kind of out of his budget right now. He'd saved up so long for the L200."

Seb looked away. It didn't sound like Lavinia had forgiven him yet. He felt a light tap on his arm and looked up to see Lavinia watching him.

"Dad says I have to forgive you, that you apologised and we have to move on," she stated, not looking particularly happy with the idea. She paused. "But you can understand why I'm still mad inside," she continued wryly.

Seb kicked a stone. "I'm kinda mad with myself too," he muttered. "I don't know why I did it."

"I don't know either!" Lavinia exclaimed, shaking her head. She smiled slightly. "But we'll not mention it again."

Seb walked around the blue truck. "I like this one," he said, approvingly.

"You may start saving up!" Lavinia laughed.

Seb stopped. He reached out a finger and rubbed a spot just behind the wheel on the passenger's side. It looked like a streak of dirt. He knelt down. There seemed to be something caught in the mud flap. Strange.

"Hey!" a voice called. "What are you at? Hands off that truck. It's brand new and I don't want you scratching it." Barry came wobbling over as fast as his short legs would carry him.

Seb stood up as Barry approached. His unnaturally dark, oily, slick-backed hair glistened in the afternoon sunshine. His eyes flashed with barely restrained anger... and something else. Seb was puzzled. Barry's reaction made no sense. He made his way back to Uncle Matt, who was still looking at the jeep.

"Well, Seb, what do you think?" he asked.

Seb shrugged. "It's okay," he replied.

"It'll do the job," Matt said. "Right, Barry, we'll take this one."

"Great!" Barry grinned, rubbing his pudgy hands together. "Come on inside and we'll get a few signatures."

"Dad," asked Lavinia on the way home. "What's a brand new truck doing in a second-hand dealership?"

"What truck, Vinnie?"

"The Ford Ranger we were looking at. The blue one."

"Oh, yes, I saw that one. Nice truck! But how do you know it was new?"

"Barry said it was brand new," Seb answered.

"It's likely an ex-demonstrator model. Barry's prone to a bit of exaggeration," Matt chuckled. "He can be very protective of his vehicles."

"You can say that again!" Seb exclaimed. "I thought he was going to have a heart attack when he saw me touching it."

"You *touched* it?" Lavinia said. "It's a wonder he didn't have you arrested!"

"I thought I saw something on it, like dirt."

"Hardly likely, Seb," said Matt. "Maybe a bit of polish that hasn't been wiped off properly or something."

Seb shrugged. That was likely all it was. But if so, what was that look on Barry's face? And what exactly had been caked on the mud flap? Was there something he was trying to hide?

Seb fell into bed, exhausted. They had come back from the dealership to a full spread of tea and cake, before going out to do the evening milking. This time he had been fully prepared for the cows, and while their size still took him by surprise, he was beginning to appreciate the large animals. Uncle Matt had sent Lavinia to feed the heifers and asked Seb to help him in the milking parlour instead. Again, it had been another eye opening experience and he wasn't sure about standing so close to the heavy hooves and strong tails. He also hadn't realised that they continued to answer the call of nature while in the parlour, and he had a couple of near misses. Uncle Matt had called, "Look out!" just before the mushy, smelly greenish-brown substance splatted right where Seb had been standing. But, despite this, he had enjoyed his experience. The warmth, the contented lowing of the cows, the hum and rhythmic chug-chug of the milking machine and the sight of the warm, creamy milk splashing into the jars overhead. Seb was fascinated by it all. Uncle Matt had also taken time to teach him, letting him wipe off the cows' teats using paper towels and showing him the best way to put on the clusters. He had even let him put that morning's tractor handling lesson into practice when it came to scraping down the area where the cows had been waiting to be milked.

Heavy rain had started to fall just as they were finishing up outside, so after a tasty dinner of mince pie and chunky, home cooked chips, followed by apple pie and ice-cream, the family had sat down to a competitive game of Monopoly. Seb was shocked to discover that Aunt Karen was actually a savvy business woman, who raked in more Monopoly money than the rest of them put together!

He yawned and stretched. Hard work and fresh air meant he wouldn't have any trouble sleeping and another busy day was ahead tomorrow.

Dad was bearing down on him, one large fist raised and a look of fury in his eyes. "Come here, you miserable excuse for a son! How dare you?!" he screamed.

Seb tried to run, but his legs felt like lead. Dad was moving closer.

"You pitiful, useless, worthless...!" He loomed over Seb.

Seb cowered and braced himself for the blow...

Seb sat bolt upright in bed. His heart was pounding and he was drenched in sweat. Where was he?

Gradually, his eyes acclimatised to the darkness and his breathing slowed. He was safe. He was at Uncle Matt and Aunt Karen's, at the farm. Dad was miles away back in Belfast. He pushed back the covers and stood up on shaky legs.

He couldn't get away from Dad. Even in his dreams he was there, taunting him, sneering at him, despising him. Was it a mistake to think he would ever be worth anything? Enough to make someone proud? Or was he destined to be a hated, good-for-nothing waster. Kind of like his dad.

He shook himself and tiptoed to the window. Slipping behind the heavy curtain, he sat on the deep windowsill, looking out into the black night. The rain had stopped and it was all still and silent; the trees silhouetted against a moonless sky. He could hear cows lowing in a nearby field. *Strange*, he thought. *I'd have thought cows would know to go to sleep in the dark.* The lowing increased in volume and he could hear a rattle of metal, followed by some clattering, a few bangs, and finally an engine starting. What was going on? Was this a usual time to move cattle? Was Uncle Matt making use of sleepless hours? Should he go and check if he needed help?

As he listened, he realised the sound was coming from the fields across the road. Seb wasn't sure who owned those fields. He knew it wasn't Uncle Matt. He had mentioned earlier that, unusually, all his ground was on this side of the road, so Seb could help with tractor work in any of his fields, but never have to be on the road. So it must be a neighbouring farmer. But why move cattle at this time? Maybe they were more placid at night, or the farmer had a long journey and needed to make an early start, or...

Suddenly, the window was illuminated in light. Seb froze and shrank back against the window frame. The light seemed to be coming from a vehicle in the field opposite the house. He watched as the lights approached the gateway, before slowing to a crawl. He could hear the growl and whine of an engine revving. The vehicle seemed to be struggling to exit the field. The lights shifted to one side and he heard a shout above the noise. After a few minutes it slowly made its way out the gateway and stopped until a dark figure shut the gate, and then moved off slowly down the road.

Seb watched the vehicle move out of sight, then sighed and went back to bed. What did he know about moving cattle?

Yawning again, he fell asleep.

Chapter Nine

Seb woke early with the ringing of the phone. He hurriedly dressed and padded downstairs. He hoped to be able to help with the milking this morning.

Uncle Matt was standing in the kitchen, his boilersuit pulled to his waist, phone to his ear.

"You definitely looked everywhere? There are no holes in the hedge where they could have escaped?"

Matt listened, running his free hand through his thick hair until it stood on end.

"All right, Tommy, give me a minute and I'll meet you there."

He pressed a button on the phone and threw it on the table. "Tommy thinks he's had some cattle stolen during the night," he told Seb.

Seb's stomach dropped. "Where were they?" he asked.

"The field directly opposite us," Matt said. "Tommy owns the ground from their house right up to here. Come with me; I'm heading down to take a look."

Seb jammed his feet into his wellies and grabbed the coat from the peg behind the office door. He ran to catch up with Matt, who was already partway down the lane.

Seb felt sick. It hadn't been a bored farmer deciding to move his cows around. It had been someone stealing Tommy's cattle. Kind, gentle Tommy.

"They were five of his best heifers," Matt explained, when Seb caught up. "If they've been stolen, and it looks like they were, those boys knew what they were after. They'll be over the border and have the eartags changed by now."

The county where the McRoss family lived bordered the Republic of Ireland. Border patrols and checkpoints were a thing of the past, and people... and animals... could move freely from Northern Ireland, part of the United Kingdom, to the Republic. While the freedom was welcomed by many, it also gave rise for opportunity for criminal activity.

Tommy was standing at the gate, shoulders bowed, looking at the remaining ten animals who were clustered around a trough a few feet from the gate. He looked up as Matt and Seb approached, a perplexed look on his old, wrinkled face.

"Definitely gone, Tommy?" Matt asked.

Tommy shook his head. "Looks like it," he said. "I checked the hedge and there's nowhere they could have got out. But look," he pointed at the ground, "they seem to have had a bit o' bother gettin' out o' the field."

The part of the field nearest the gateway sloped away from the road before levelling out, then rising again on a slight incline.

"They've obviously gone into the field to turn, or to get off the road, but they've certainly made a right mess," Uncle Matt said, looking at the churned up ground, and the dirty tyre tracks leaving the field.

"That's why I always use the back lane if I need to drive into this field," Tommy said. "It's a steep wee bit, and always gets that waterlogged. It's a wile pity nobody was driving past at the time."

Seb cleared his throat. He was kicking himself for not alerting someone when he saw the lights.

"I saw lights last night," he said, softly.

Matt and Tommy swung around to face him. "What do you mean?" Matt asked.

"I woke up in the middle of the night and went to the window. I heard cows and banging noises, then I saw lights coming out of the field."

"What time was this at?" Tommy questioned.

"I don't know," Seb replied, downcast. "I didn't think to look at the clock. I didn't know this was your field, Tommy, and I thought somebody was just moving cows. I don't know what's normal here." He bit his lip and kicked at a clump of grass. "I'm sorry," he added.

Uncle Matt patted him on the shoulder. "Don't worry about it, Seb," he said. "Nobody else heard a thing, so you did better than us, but just so you know, farmers move cattle during the day." He smiled at Seb.

"Well, we better call the police," Tommy said, pulling out his mobile phone, holding it at arm's length and squinting at it. He handed it to Matt. "Here, Matt son, you do it, I can't see it that well without my glasses."

Investigating the case of the missing cattle wasn't high on the local police force's priority list that morning, so Madge made scrambled eggs for breakfast while they waited for them to arrive.

"I can't believe it, Matt," she said, shaking her head as she cracked eggs into a big, white enamel bowl. "The rotters, stealin' our heifers. Tommy was for takin' thon ones tae the market this week! And tae think nobody heard a thing! Apart fae Seb here. Wile pity ye didn't say, son, but I s'pose ye weren't tae know. But if I could get me hands on thon boys…" She beat the eggs viciously. Seb made a mental note to never get on the wrong side of Madge. "They're likely well across the border by now. This is no on, they'll have tae be stopped! They can't go and steal innocent folks' cattle that they've worked hard tae rear." She added a good shake of salt and pepper, then tipped the mixture into a large saucepan on the stove.

Tommy was sitting in his chair by the stove, looking downcast. Seb felt sorry for him. He obviously put a lot of work into his farm and to know that someone else – who didn't deserve it – was going to benefit while Tommy lost out, was making Seb increasingly angry.

If he was angry before, he was livid by the time the police officers eventually left. "Uncle Matt, why aren't they doing more to find out who did it?" he asked indignantly after Tommy took them home in his old grey Defender.

"They've come across these situations before, Seb," Matt answered, rubbing his forehead wearily. "By now the heifers are likely over the border and there's nothing they can do that'll prove who did it."

"But couldn't they check fingerprints on the gate and look at tyre marks?"

Matt chuckled dryly. "You watch too much TV, Seb! The police have plenty to do. Investigating stolen cattle isn't something they are likely to spend time and resources on when it's unlikely to result in convictions."

"But it's so unfair!" exclaimed Seb. "Tommy works hard!"

"I know he does," replied Uncle Matt. "But there are bad men around, ones who don't care about the consequences to a good old man like Tommy."

"They don't deserve to get away with it!" Seb declared. "It's wrong!"

Matt regarded him thoughtfully. "Why do you say that?" he asked.

Hadn't Uncle Matt been listening? "Stealing is wrong, everyone knows that!"

"How does everyone know that?"

Seb wasn't sure what Uncle Matt was getting at. "You just *know* it's wrong! It's not fair to just take things from people."

"So did anyone ever tell you it was wrong to steal?"

"I don't know," he said. "I'm sure Mum did, but I can't remember." Was he getting at him about taking the truck again?

"Do you know that the Bible says it's wrong to steal?"

So that's what Uncle Matt was angling towards. "I don't really care what the Bible says. We know that anyway; we don't need a book to tell us what we should do."

"So, Seb," asked Uncle Matt mildly, "did evolution put that knowledge of right and wrong inside us?"

Seb shrugged. "I guess it did. Or it has evolved with us over time." It wasn't something he'd thought a lot about.

"But where do people's standards of right and wrong come from? Who decided stealing is wrong? What about people cheating on their husbands or wives? What about murder? No one doubts that that is definitely wrong, but how do we know that?"

Seb frowned. He wished Uncle Matt wasn't so logical all the time!

"You know, a human being is not just a collection of cells," Uncle Matt continued. "We all know that there are things that we ought to do that may be uncomfortable or difficult for us, like going out of our way to help an old lady cross the road, or something bigger, such as donating a kidney to someone we love. And there are other things that we know we shouldn't do, even if we think it would make us happy. Seb, evolution can't explain that. Atheism doesn't know, and in many cases doesn't care. In fact, if you follow atheism to its conclusion then there is no such thing as right and wrong."

Seb looked away. He didn't like what he was hearing, but what Uncle Matt was saying was making sense.

"Do you want to hear what I believe?" Uncle Matt asked.

"I think you're going to tell me anyway!"

Uncle Matt laughed. "Absolutely!" he said. "Doesn't it make so much more sense to believe that God has set the standard and given us a conscience? The Bible is God's word to us and gives us His standards, which, by the way, we can't ever meet on our own. That's why He gave His Son, Jesus Christ, to die on the cross to make us right with Him."

"You really believe that, don't you? That whole Jesus business?"

"Of course I do, Seb. When Someone changes your life and gives you a reason to live, well, you know He's real all right!" Uncle Matt smiled.

Seb scuffed the ground with the toe of his welly. What was he living for? He thought of his life in Belfast - an endless round of school, hanging around with his friends, going to bed, getting up, school... Life seemed so empty if that was all there was to it. He actually felt envious of Uncle Matt, having a reason to live. But that was silly, wasn't it? Sure religion was just a crutch? He frowned. Uncle Matt didn't exactly fit the mould of someone who needed a crutch, though...

"Come on, Seb," said Uncle Matt. "We better get inside and get some lunch. We've the jeep to pick up this afternoon."

"Get on okay with the milking this morning, Vinnie?" Matt asked his daughter over lunch.

She nodded and swallowed her mouthful of chicken pie. "Joe said to be sure and tell you that a couple of the cows are looking a bit lame. He thinks we need that hoofcare man... what's his name?"

"Grant Everson?"

"Yes, him. Anyway, Joe thinks we need him out again." She paused. "He was a bit quiet this morning. I think he'd a headache."

Aunt Karen shook her head. "Joe's a nice guy," she said. "But I do wish he wasn't so fond of his big nights out."

"We don't know for sure that he was out last night, Karen," Matt said mildly, reaching for another slice of wheaten bread.

"I know that, but sadly, with Joe, that's the usual reason for a headache first thing in the morning. I just wish he would realise that the nights out don't bring him any true satisfaction. Once one is over, he can't wait for the next one."

"We'll keep praying for him, Karen." Matt smiled at his wife across the table.

Seb looked down at his plate. He couldn't help compare his home to this one. Here, there was love and contentment, no angry words or threats. Would believing in God really make so much difference to a home? Surely people could be good without believing in God. Yet Uncle Matt's beliefs seemed to make a difference to the way he treated those around him. And even if they were deluded and there really was no God, at the very least it certainly wasn't doing anyone in this family any harm.

Chapter Ten

It was a tight squeeze in the back of the little red car. Martha's booster seat seemed to take up half the back seat and Uncle Matt's legs were so long that the front passenger's seat had to be pushed back as far as it could go so he could fit. Aunt Karen was a menace behind the wheel! Seb was pressed against the door, and every corner they flew around Lavinia struggled not to land on top of him.

"Mum!" she finally exclaimed.

"Yes, dear?"

"Could you *please* slow down? I'm going to land on Seb and *kill* him if you keep rallying around those corners like that."

Uncle Matt chuckled. "Your mum doesn't like to waste one second of time, Vinnie. You should know that by now."

Aunt Karen glanced at him indignantly. "Do you mean to say you don't like my driving?"

Uncle Matt smirked. "I never said the words!"

"But you thought them!" Aunt Karen stood on the brakes and pulled over to the side of the road. "So you can all get out and walk, since this is such a terrible journey for you!"

Uncle Matt threw back his head and laughed. "Aw, Karen!" he said. "Come on, we need to get this jeep!"

Aunt Karen turned and looked at him sternly, but Seb could detect a twinkle in her eye. "So are you happy with my driving, or will you walk?"

Uncle Matt threw up his hands. "Okay, okay!" he said. "We'll keep quiet, won't we, Vinnie?"

"Hmm!" Lavinia pretended to think about it for a few seconds. "All right, we'll not say a word."

Aunt Karen pulled away again. Matt glanced around and winked at Lavinia, then at the next corner they both put their hands in the air as if they were on a rollercoaster and let the momentum of the car send them off balance. Thankfully it sent Lavinia towards Martha, where her booster seat was protecting her. She giggled and put her own hands in the air.

Lavinia nudged Seb. "Join in," she mouthed.

"No way," he mouthed back. This was seriously not cool!

"Aw, go on."

Martha leaned forward to look around Lavinia. "Please, Seb," she whispered.

Seb shrugged and put his hands in the air. Karen rounded another bend and they all fell to Seb's side of the car. It was followed quickly by a bend in the other direction and he fell against Lavinia.

Aunt Karen shook her head, a slight smile playing on her lips. "You lot are crazy!" she said.

Seb grinned. It was a crazy thing to do, but it felt good, being crazy with other people. He really was beginning to feel like one of the family. He didn't think he would care if he never lived in Belfast again.

Aunt Karen pulled into the dealership and Seb, Lavinia and Uncle Matt got out. Spinning out of the carpark, she headed on her way to do the weekly grocery shop.

The others walked towards the small square building, at the far side of the yard, which served as the office. Seb nudged Lavinia. "He must have sold the Ranger," he said.

Lavinia looked behind her to the spot where the blue truck had been. "You're right, it's gone!"

"I'm not surprised," added Uncle Matt. "Barry doesn't usually have vehicles just as new as that one. I'd imagine it generated quite a bit of interest."

They had reached the office. Uncle Matt pushed open the frosted glass door and stepped in. A large desk, covered with piles of paper and a mug of cold coffee, served as the reception counter. Two grey fabric covered seats sat in front of it, and a large, black leather chair behind it. Filing cabinets, drawers lying open, stretched along the wall from the far side of the desk to the corner of the room. Lavinia rubbed her finger along the edge of the desk and wrinkled her nose in disgust. "Mum would be horrified," she exclaimed. "Look at this dust!"

"Sshh, Vinnie," whispered Uncle Matt. "It's not polite to point out the shortcomings in people's cleaning habits!"

"Well, it doesn't exactly look like he's here, anyway," replied Lavinia.

"He's maybe working round the back," Seb suggested. "Should we go and see?"

"I suppose we could," Uncle Matt said. They pushed open the door and stepped back into the bright July sunshine. A large blue wooden gate stood open to their left and they could see another yard and a shed. There still was no sign of Barry so they headed in the direction of the shed. A flash of blue caught Seb's eye. Tucked into the corner of the yard sat the Ford Ranger, but not in the pristine condition it had been in yesterday. Today it had muck over the alloys, along the bottom of the doors and splatted in streaks up the side. A thick rim of mud lined the large tyres. As they stepped over for a closer look, Barry appeared from the shed. As he noticed them, Seb was convinced a fleeting look of panic crossed his large flabby face, but he quickly recovered and wobbled over to them.

"Well, Matt," he said jovially. "You're here for your jeep."

"That's right," Matt answered. He pointed to the Ranger. "We thought it had sold already."

"No, no, not yet," Barry chuckled. "Although I'm sure it'll not be long. Nice vehicle. Even nicer than your L200, I'd say. It's been out for a test drive; I'm going to get it all cleaned up again later."

"Someone has been testing the four wheel drive by the looks of it," Matt said.

Barry gave a dry laugh and started off for the front door of the office. "You know what people are like nowadays," he said vaguely. "Now, let's get this paperwork sorted and get you on the road again."

The paperwork took ages, but as Lavinia and Seb opened the door, thinking they would wander around the cars until the men were finished with the finer details of signing over a vehicle, Barry looked up and shook his head. "We don't allow kids to run around unsupervised," he said with a greasy smile.

Lavinia's mouth fell open. "How dare you? We aren't children!" she exclaimed.

Matt looked up at her. "Lavinia," he said. "Sit down. We're nearly done."

Lavinia looked like she wanted to argue her case, then shrugged and dropped into the free seat. Seb watched Barry. He seemed visibly relieved. By now Seb was pretty certain he was hiding something. *Could it be...?* He couldn't wait to get back to the farm.

It was almost time for the evening milking when they arrived back at Cherryhill Farm. Uncle Matt had had a list of things he needed from Harvey's. What Seb hadn't realised was that Andrew Harvey, the owner, was an old friend of Uncle Matt's. It was a slack day and Andrew seemed in no hurry to get back to work. Lavinia's inspection of her appearance in the mirror in the sun visor as they drove into Harvey's carpark made sense when a tall, ginger haired boy, who looked to be a year or two older than them, appeared from a store room at the back. Andrew introduced him as his son, Caleb. Seb was amused at the change in Lavinia, from tough, outspoken tomboy, to sweet, hair-flicking, and almost flirtatious girl.

He'd asked her about Caleb on the way home.

"Oh, he's just a friend," she'd replied dismissively.

Seb had sniggered.

"*What* are you laughing at?" she'd said sternly.

"Nothing," he'd replied, hiding his grin.

They just had time for a quick cup of tea and a scone with strawberry jam before they went out to milk.

"I was talking to Andrew when I was over at Harvey's earlier," Uncle Matt told Aunt Karen. "They said we'd have to come over for dinner some night."

"Yes, that'd be good," Aunt Karen replied. "It's been a while since we've met up. I know we see them on Sundays, but I haven't had a proper chat with Sarah in ages."

"What about you, Lavinia?" asked Seb. "Are you looking forward to going to visit your *friend*?" He raised an eyebrow.

"Oh, yes," she replied sweetly, a look of triumph in her eyes. "I always like going to visit Rebekah."

"Ah, but what about Rebekah's big brother?" Uncle Matt added.

"What about him?" she said with a sniff.

Seb laughed. "Aunt Karen, you should have seen her! She was getting all worried about her hair, and then when Caleb came out... OW! What'd you do that for?" He reached down and rubbed his shin, glaring at his cousin.

"Oh, did I kick you?" she asked innocently.

"You're right you did! And you meant to, you wee–"

"Right, Seb, if you're finished with your tea come on and we'll get these cows in," Uncle Matt interrupted, pushing his chair back and standing up.

After dinner that evening Seb carried his plate over to the sink. "I'm going a walk," he called over his shoulder. "I won't be long."

He stuck his feet into his boots and headed down the lane. He heard footsteps after him and quickened his pace. He didn't want company. What he intended to do he'd rather do alone. The footsteps sped up. "Seb," Lavinia called. "Wait for me!"

Seb sighed. He wasn't going to be able to shake her off. He slowed down.

"Where are you going?" Lavinia asked, falling into step beside him.

"For a walk."

"I know. You said that, but where?"

He shrugged. "Just down the road a bit."

"Can I come with you?"

"Do I have a choice?" he asked wryly.

"Nope!" Lavinia grinned. "I'm sorry for kicking you earlier, but you shouldn't tell tales."

"I was telling the truth! You really do have it bad for that Caleb guy, don't you?"

Lavinia turned red and looked away. "Let's talk about something else," she said.

Seb laughed. "What's your problem with just admitting it? In fact, why don't you just tell him yourself?"

"What?!" Lavinia spun around to look at him, eyes wide. "I'd *never* do that!"

"So you do like him!"

"Please, Seb, let's not discuss this," she pleaded.

They had reached the end of the lane. Seb could see the churned up ground and tyre tracks in the gateway. There was only one way he was going to be able to inspect them, and that was if he told Lavinia what he was doing.

"You saw the lights and you didn't get Dad?" she asked, dumbfounded at Seb's stupidity.

"Well, I didn't know it wasn't normal! Anyway, I'll know better the next time."

"Let's hope there is no 'next time'," replied Lavinia, shaking her head.

Seb bent down to inspect the ground. The tracks seemed quite wide, but there was no visible tyre print. He climbed the gate and dropped over the other side. He felt a crunching beneath his feet and looked down.

Scattered on the gored up ground were shards of clear plastic.

Chapter Eleven

"How far is it to Barry's dealership?" Seb asked, hurriedly.

Lavinia wrinkled her nose at him. "About ten miles," she answered. "What do you want to go there for?"

He pointed at the ground. "I want to check that Ranger."

"Seb," Lavinia said, incredulously, "you don't think that Barry is into cattle rustling. He doesn't look the type."

"Have you ever seen a cattle rustler before to know what they look like?"

"I suppose not," she conceded. "But how do you propose we get there?

"Um... can we ride the bikes?"

Lavinia threw back her head and laughed. "Oh, sure," she said. "A twenty mile round trip at eight o'clock at night! I can see Dad agreeing to that!"

"We don't need to tell him," Seb replied.

Lavinia raised an eyebrow. "I don't think you should pull any more stunts for a while. Dad has been very longsuffering with you, but I wouldn't push it!"

"Well, smarty, do you have any better ideas?"

"Why don't we just ask Dad to take us?"

Seb shook his head. "I don't think he'd see the point of going. He certainly wouldn't want to snoop around Barry's yard anyway. Don't you know anyone else who could take us? Who else can drive round here?"

Lavinia suddenly became preoccupied with her fingernails.

"Lavinia?"

"Um... the only person I can think of is... Caleb," she finished in a soft voice.

Aunt Karen frowned. "You're going where?" she asked.

"To get ice-cream in the town," Lavinia replied.

"And how do you intend to get to the town? On your bikes?" asked Uncle Matt, a little sarcastically.

"No," replied Lavinia. "Rebekah and Caleb are coming too. Caleb's driving," she added, as casually as she could.

"Caleb?!" Aunt Karen exclaimed. "I'm not sure about this at all!"

"Aw, Aunt Karen," said Seb. "I'll be there. I'll stay with them, make sure they behave, and don't go sneaking off somewhere to..."

"SEB!" Lavinia spun around, red-faced.

He held up his hands in mock surrender. "Oh, okay. You *can* sneak off together, then!"

Lavinia sputtered at Seb. She flapped her arms up and down and finally gave up. She had no idea why she had ever agreed to Seb's hare-brained plan.

Uncle Matt chuckled. "Aw, Karen, sure, we'll let them go tonight. But, Vinnie," he stood up and put an arm round his daughter, "you know the rules. No boyfriend for a couple of years yet."

They went outside to wait for Caleb and Rebekah.

"You know, that really wasn't helpful, what you said to Mum," she told Seb.

Seb snorted with laughter. "I don't know what your problem is. And what's all this old-fashioned stuff about not allowing you to have a boyfriend yet? Do they want you to be a nun or something?"

Lavinia shook her head. "They think I'm too young."

Seb frowned. "Too young? That's crazy!"

Lavinia shrugged. "Maybe. But that's their rule. I think they don't want to see me get hurt."

Seb was about to reply when he heard a car coming up the lane. "I think they're here. Lavinia, don't say too much about what I'm looking for. Just pretend we're admiring the Ranger again."

Lavinia looked unsure, but hadn't time to argue. The red Corsa pulled into the yard. A tall, blonde girl hopped out of the passenger seat and slid her seat forward, then climbed into the back. Lavinia clambered in after her, and Seb slid the seat back into place. As he stepped in, Uncle Matt appeared at the back door of the house. "Evening, Caleb!" he called.

Caleb put down his window. "Evening, Matt," he said. "How's it going?"

"Grand," answered Matt. "Don't know how you got roped into doing taxi, but drive carefully and don't be late back."

Caleb grinned and gave him a thumbs up. "No bother, Matt!" he called as they drove out of the yard.

Uncle Matt smiled and shook his head, before waving and going back into the house.

"So, Seb," said Caleb. "Good to see you again. How're you getting on at Cherryhill?"

Seb nodded. How *was* he getting on? Between nearly getting mauled by an over-friendly cow, crashing and rolling a pickup truck, learning to drive a tractor, unknowingly seeing cattle being rustled and trying to figure out why Barry, the car salesman, was acting so shifty, he certainly hadn't suffered from boredom!

"Fine," he answered. "It's a lot different from Belfast."

"I'm sure it is," replied Caleb. "Oh," he jabbed a thumb in the direction of the back seat, "that's my sister Rebekah. Her and Vinnie are best friends."

Seb glanced into the back seat.

Rebekah was in the middle of a lengthy description of the purchases of a shopping trip earlier that day. Her eyes were wide and animated and she was gesturing wildly as she described her latest clothes. She stopped when she saw Seb looking around.

"Hi, Rebekah," he said.

"Hi, Seb," she answered, brushing a honey-coloured strand away from her eyes.

"Nice to meet you."

"You too," she giggled.

"So you're Lavinia's friend? How in the world do you cope?"

She nodded solemnly. "It's not easy," she answered, "but I try my best."

"Hey!" exclaimed Lavinia. "That's not fair!"

"No, it's not!" added Caleb, adjusting his rear-view mirror to see Lavinia. "I think Vinnie has more to cope with than Rebekah does."

Lavinia raised her chin. "Thank you, Caleb!" she said.

"Welcome," he replied, winking at her in the mirror.

Seb chuckled. "Oh, Aunt Karen, wait till you hear about this," he chortled.

Lavinia reached around between the door and the seat and poked him hard in the ribs. Then, ignoring him, she turned to Rebekah and resumed their earlier conversation.

The ice-cream shop closed at ten thirty and they only left after the staff began to give a strong hint by beginning to put the shutter down.

Seb had enjoyed his time with Caleb and Rebekah. Caleb had a wicked sense of humour and Seb couldn't remember the last time he'd laughed so hard. But while the time was good, this wasn't the reason why they had come to town.

"Caleb, there's this amazing Ford Ranger at the second-hand dealership. We should call out and see it," Seb suggested.

Caleb looked at his watch. "What time is 'late', Vinnie?" he asked.

Lavinia shrugged. "Probably after midnight," she answered.

Caleb smiled. "Are you sure?" he asked. "I'd hate to get into your dad's bad books!"

"Well, maybe we should head back soon," she conceded. "But it's still early."

"Time enough to check out the Ranger," added Seb.

Caleb didn't need much persuasion. They piled back into the car and headed out the road to the dealership.

"Park here," Seb instructed, pointing to a lay-by opposite.

They clambered out of the car and crossed the road. The gates were shut but the wall was low enough to easily step over.

"Where is it?" asked Caleb. "I don't see it."

Seb glanced around. It wasn't fully dark yet, and it was obvious in the pale light that the Ranger wasn't on show. There were two options. Either it was still in the yard, or it was out for another 'test drive'. Seb wasn't going to leave until he found out which it was.

"Follow me," he said, walking towards the gate to the side of the office.

"Seb," called Lavinia. "You're crazy! What if he has CCTV?"

He shrugged, but pulled up the hood of his sweatshirt anyway. Reaching the gate, he reached through the opening to slide the bolt back, but it was padlocked shut. Standing back he looked up. Too high. He'd never be able to climb it.

Turning, he walked around to the other side of the office. A wall ran from the office towards the back of the property. This was lower.

"Caleb." He waved the tall young man over. Caleb glanced around furtively, then shrugged and put up his hood as well.

"What is it, Seb?" he asked.

"Here, give me a leg up."

"You aren't going to jump over that wall," Caleb said in disbelief.

"Why not?" asked Seb. "I need to see if it's still here."

"But, Seb," Caleb protested, "I don't need to see it that badly. It's likely sold or something."

"I don't think so," he replied. "Come on, Caleb, I just want a wee look."

Caleb shook his head, but held out his hands for Seb to stand on. He pulled himself onto the wall and looked down. "There she is!" he exclaimed. "Can you climb up, Caleb?"

Caleb grasped the top of the wall and pulled himself up. "Yes, very good, Seb," he said. "She looks good, from what I can see of her from this angle, but can we go now? I don't like prowling around like this. If we get caught..."

Seb jumped off the wall into the yard.

"Seb! What are you doing?" Caleb was horrified.

Seb began to walk around the truck. As he reached the front bonnet a bright light flooded the yard.

Caleb jumped off the wall back into the forecourt and hissed, "Seb, get back. He likely has CCTV or some sort of burglar alarm!"

Seb ignored him and continued his inspection of the truck. It had been cleaned up, the mud was gone, the paintwork was shining and the tyres a deep black again. But as he reached the passenger wing mirror, it was obvious why the truck was still hidden away.

The indicator cover, at the very tip of the chrome wing mirror, was gone.

"I can't believe you did that!" Rebekah exclaimed as they crossed the road to the car.

Seb shrugged. "It was only a sensor light," he said. "A cat can set one of those off easily. No one will suspect a thing."

"Unless he has CCTV," countered Caleb. "And then we've had it."

They reached the car and Rebekah climbed into the back behind Caleb. Seb beat Lavinia to the opposite door and clambered in beside Rebekah. Lavinia hesitated, but Seb pulled the passenger seat into place. Caleb seemed rattled, so maybe some female company would help calm him down. And Seb's own situation wasn't so bad either!

Seb's plan seemed to work. Caleb and Lavinia kept up a steady stream of quiet chatter the whole way home and when he dropped them off he seemed to have forgiven Seb for his crazy action.

Aunt Karen met them at the door. "What time do you call this?" she demanded, tapping her watchless wrist.

"Two hairs past a freckle," giggled Lavinia.

Aunt Karen frowned. "None of that smart talk, girl!" she said. "This is too late! It's nearly eleven thirty!"

Seb swung round to look at Lavinia. She had said after twelve was late. He had thought twelve was still rather early, so he was surprised at the frosty reception they were getting.

"Nobody told us what time to be home, Aunt Karen," Seb said.

"Lavinia ought to know," she replied. "We all get up early so we need to get to bed at a decent time." She shook her head. "Well, you're home safely anyway. Go on, I'll lock up."

As they made their way up the stairs, Lavinia whispered to Seb, "See anything?"

"Yes," he replied. "It's what I thought. The indicator cover is missing. I think they're using the Ranger for their cattle rustling."

"What do we do now?" asked Lavinia.

"We try to stop them."

Lavinia stopped dead. "You aren't serious!"

"Sssh! Your mum's coming. We'll talk in the morning."

Lavinia headed to the right into her room, and Seb rounded the hallway to his room at the front of the house. He got ready for bed and cleaned his teeth, then pulled back the green blanket and quilt and climbed into the bed. But it was a long time before he was able to sleep.

Chapter Twelve

Seb woke on Friday morning feeling as if he hadn't slept at all. He had tossed and turned for a long time, but, try as he might, he couldn't come up with any sort of feasible plan to track down the cattle rustlers. There were just too many unknowns, including where they would next strike, and when. He certainly couldn't keep prowling around Barry's dealership; Seb wouldn't put it past Barry to call the police if he appeared again, especially if he had recognised him from the CCTV footage. He would simply have to keep his eyes and ears open, and wait.

"Vinnie, if you're taking that heifer to the show, you'll need to get to work. You have just about two weeks," Uncle Matt told his daughter after a filling breakfast of porridge and honey.

Lavinia downed her orange juice in one gulp and carried her bowl and glass over to the sink. "Yep," she said. "I'll work on her this morning."

Uncle Matt reached for his Bible. "You can go and get her once we've done our morning Bible reading."

Seb sighed. He guessed he would just have to get used to hearing the Bible read. Uncle Matt obviously didn't make exceptions for anyone, not even atheists! If you got your breakfast at Cherryhill, you listened to the Bible. He wondered if Joe's speedy exit straight after milking was really to do with helping his neighbour with the silage, or with escaping Uncle Matt's sermon for the day.

"We missed the reading yesterday with being at Tommy's. Did you read the next psalm?" Matt asked Karen.

"Yes," she replied. "It's Psalm 22 today."

Uncle Matt cleared his throat. "Okay. Psalm 22," he said, and began to read.

Seb slumped in his chair and looked out the window. He could see Jess sniffing around the yard, before curling up in a patch of sunshine and falling asleep. The fridge hummed and a fly buzzed lazily around the room.

Gradually, the words which Uncle Matt was reading caught Seb's attention. He sat up straighter. This wasn't really like the last Psalm he'd heard Uncle Matt read. This one sounded like someone was speaking in great distress. Whatever was going on here?

He listened, intrigued.

" '…A reproach of men, and despised by the people. All those who see Me ridicule Me…' "

Seb knew what it was like to be despised and ridiculed. It wasn't a nice feeling.

" '... Many bulls have surrounded Me; strong bulls of Bashan have encircled Me. They gape at Me with their mouths, like a raging and roaring lion. I am poured out like water, and all My bones are out of joint; My heart is like wax; it has melted within Me. My strength is dried up like a potsherd, and My tongue clings to My jaws...' "

Seb thought back to his experience with Mirabelle. An inquisitive cow was terrifying enough, but to be surrounded with bulls...! Whoever was speaking was obviously going to die.

" '... dogs have surrounded Me; the congregation of the wicked has enclosed Me. They pierced My hands and My feet; I can count all My bones. They look and stare at Me. They divide My garments among them, and for My clothing they cast lots...' "

Seb listened intently as Uncle Matt read the remaining verses and lowered the Bible to the table. "A precious part of God's Word," he said.

Aunt Karen nodded in agreement.

"Do you understand this Psalm, Seb?"

Seb shook his head. "Who is it speaking about?" he asked.

"It was written by David, a king of Israel, but it is actually prophetic, speaking of what would happen around 1000 years later. Let me read you a couple of verses from the New Testament. John chapter 19, verses 17 and 18 – 'And He, bearing His cross, went out to a place called the Place of a Skull, which is called in Hebrew, Golgotha, where they crucified Him, and two others with Him, one on either side, and Jesus in the centre.' "

Jesus! Was that really who this Psalm was speaking of?

Uncle Matt looked at Seb, his finger marking the place on the page. "What was crucifixion? Do you know?"

Seb shrugged. "Something to do with a cross?"

"Yes, you're right," Uncle Matt replied. "It was a Roman method of putting criminals to death, where they nailed the person alive to a cross. It was a most brutal and horrible way to die. We read in Psalm 22, 'They pierced My hands and My feet.' It is so obvious that the reference to piercing of hands and feet refers to Roman crucifixion, even though this was long before the Romans were around."

"But it says that there were two other men crucified as well. If they crucified lots of people, how do we know that it wasn't talking about any of them?"

Uncle Matt smiled. "So how do you explain the part which reads, 'They divide My garments among them'? Let's turn to John 19 again, this time verses 23 and 24 – 'Then the soldiers, when they had crucified Jesus, took His garments and made four parts, to each soldier a part, and also the tunic. Now the tunic was without seam, woven from the top in one piece. They said therefore among themselves, "Let us not tear it, but cast lots for it, whose it shall be," that the Scripture might be fulfilled which says: "They divided My garments among them, and for My clothing they cast lots." ' You know, Seb, the dividing of the garments is not just a coincidence. We don't read of them gambling for the other men's clothes. These Roman soldiers didn't know that what they were doing was fulfilling prophecy. They wouldn't have known the Jewish scriptures, and even if they did, they certainly wouldn't have been interested in trying to fulfil them."

"But how do you even know that Jesus was a real person, and it's not just a made up story?"

"Ah, Seb! That's a very big question! There are a few ways I could answer that, but I guess you're most likely interested in the historical answer. Of course, there is a lot written in the Bible about Jesus Christ, but there are also other references to Him in writings by ancient non-Christian historians. And we have the gospels themselves, the first four books of the New Testament, written by four different writers. These are the books about Jesus' life, death and resurrection, and time and again things have been discovered which confirm many things these books say. Places in Jerusalem which were buried for years have been excavated, confirming that the writers were historically accurate."

"We also have to remember, Seb," added Aunt Karen. "That the Bible is not just written by men, but it is God's word. God told men what to write, He inspired it, so we can take it as His word to us."

"But how do you know that for sure? I mean, they could just have said that and Christians swallow it!"

Aunt Karen smiled, a twinkle in her brown eyes. "And how do you know for sure that it *isn't* God's word?"

"Well, if there's no God, then it couldn't be His word!"

"But do you know for sure there's no God?" she asked.

Seb paused, then shook his head. This was a point he hadn't considered. The atheists he knew were so busy crying out about there being no evidence for God, he hadn't actually stopped to consider that they actually had no evidence to say conclusively there was no God.

"Just because we can't see something or someone doesn't mean they don't exist," added Uncle Matt. "You hadn't met us before you arrived, but you believed we existed!"

Seb reluctantly smiled. "But that's not quite the same. Mum knew you, and I always saw your Christmas card."

"But how do you know your mum wasn't making it all up, and the Christmas card just didn't appear someday all by itself?"

Lavinia and Martha giggled. It did seem very foolish when it was put like that!

"So you knew a witness and saw evidence of our existence. What about Christians who know God personally, and what about God's work evidenced in creation?"

"I suppose it depends on whether you believe that God made the world, or believe in the Big Bang and evolution."

"I would be careful, Seb, if I were you. You don't want to discount clear evidence for an unbelievable and virtually impossible theory."

Seb stared at Uncle Matt in amazement. It sounded just like something Mr Symons, his biology teacher, would say. Except Uncle Matt was looking at it from the other side of the debate.

Aunt Karen glanced at the clock above the Aga. "This is a good conversation, but I have to have Martha to the dentist by ten, so we'd need to get a move on."

Uncle Matt closed the Bible. "Okay, we'll just have a word of prayer before you go." He bowed his head and closed his eyes, and for the first time since he'd arrived at Cherryhill, Seb followed suit.

Uncle Matt put Seb to work clearing out dirty bedding from pens in the shed. Jess followed him down the yard and lay basking in a patch of sunlight in the doorway. As he worked he couldn't help but think of that morning's discussion. The way Uncle Matt and Aunt Karen talked made atheism seem illogical and crazy! Why had he never thought of these things before? And why had he allowed himself to be convinced without even looking into it for himself? Why, that was what atheists accused Christians of doing! But obviously Matt and Karen hadn't been brainwashed – they seemed to have looked into these things for themselves.

He still found it difficult to accept the existence of God, and the fact that everything was created. Surely the scientists weren't stupid and gullible! But he was starting to doubt whether evolution could have fine-tuned so exactly all the amazing processes in the human body. He paused, muck-filled graip in hand. He was starting to feel, as Uncle Matt said on his first day here, that to believe in a Creator would be easier than to believe that the universe came into being for no reason and on its own.

By the time lunchtime arrived, Seb had worked up an appetite. He had cleared out all the pens in the shed and his arms were aching. As he'd worked he had caught glimpses of Lavinia leading what looked to him like a young cow around the yard. The animal was wearing a halter and Lavinia had a hold of it right at the top, the back of her hand resting against the cheek. The heifer wasn't following along particularly well, and Lavinia seemed to be struggling to restrain her at times.

"How's the heifer doing?" asked Uncle Matt over pasta bake.

Lavinia sighed. "Not too good," she replied.

"Well, you'd better keep practicing," said Aunt Karen.

"I'm hoping to start the silage next week," commented Uncle Matt. "The forecast looks great for the first part of the week."

"How long will it take to get it done?" Seb asked.

"A few days should do it, but there are always breakdowns! Maybe more so in May when we bring out equipment that has been lying unused in the shed all winter, but farming is like that – not always straightforward!"

"Is Joe helping us again this year?" asked Lavinia, taking a big mouthful of pasta.

Uncle Matt nodded. "Yes, he's been helping one of his neighbours with his silage these days, but he'll be finished before next week. So we have Joe, Tommy, Seb, you and me. We're well covered this time."

Seb froze. He had forgotten that Uncle Matt was planning on him helping out. Suddenly, he wondered if he could do it. The others had been doing this for years, but he'd only learned how to drive a tractor a few days ago.

Aunt Karen looked across the table and smiled at his worried frown. "You'll do great, Seb," she said. "Matt says you're a natural when it comes to tractor driving."

Seb looked down at his plate. He really hoped so. He would hate to let Uncle Matt down.

Chapter Thirteen

Seb lifted the black leather-bound Bible from his bed. Aunt Karen had told him after supper that she'd left a little present for him in his room. He'd been hoping that they'd decided to give him back his smartphone, but instead he found a *Bible*!

He grinned wryly to himself. What on earth would Dad say if he knew? He flipped through its pages. It was a long book and the writing seemed to be very small. Seb wasn't too keen on reading at the best of times, so he set it on his bedside table and flopped onto the bed, hands behind his head.

Dad had always told him that the Bible was a book which was written by a bunch of men and was full of contradictions. He wondered how his dad knew that. He'd have to ask him sometime.

He thought of his mum and dad back in Belfast. He wondered if Dad was still going out drinking as much, and what sort of mood he was in. Had he hit Mum lately? For the first time since he arrived he thought of Gran. Was she still in hospital? His mind turned to his small bedroom in his house in Belfast. He looked around him – this bedroom was easily four times the size, and was so much nicer. Granted, it wasn't just how he would have chosen to decorate it;

a bit too old-lady for his liking, but having his own bathroom and a huge bed made up for that.

He wondered how his friends were passing the time. Likely spending a lot of time in the retail carpark, or smoking beside the railway line. Tyler had even boasted a few months back that he might be able to get something else to smoke if they wanted to try it. Secretly, Seb was relieved that he was here. At the time he'd been as psyched as the others at the thought of smoking dope, but after his disastrous attempt at smoking ordinary cigarettes he hadn't been so sure. And now he was here on the farm he didn't feel he needed to experience the things the others had become so excited about.

He stood up and went into the bathroom to clean his teeth. He was kept so busy these days. He knew that the summer would have dragged at home. He never looked forward to going back to school after holidays, but there was only so much hanging around with friends and watching TV that he could do. His hand stilled... he was actually *glad* he was here, and he was actually enjoying himself! Spitting out the toothpaste, he chuckled to himself. He didn't even feel like the same bitter, rebellious, hurting boy who'd stepped off the train a few days ago. And... he caught a glimpse of himself - tanned face, bright eyes - in the mirror... he didn't even look like the same person, either.

"Seb! SEB!" Aunt Karen's voice rang across the yard to where Seb was standing, watching Joe mow the fields. The field of lush green grass was being transformed to long, straight rows on a pale yellow surface and the smell of cut grass filled his nostrils. He turned to see her jogging across the yard and ran to meet her.

"Your dad is on the phone," she told him.

Seb's heart sank. His dad was the last person he wanted to speak to right now. Aunt Karen saw his reluctance and put a hand on his shoulder. "Did he say what he wanted?" he asked.

"He didn't say," she replied. "I'd think he just wants a chat to see how you're doing."

Seb said nothing. He knew what his dad was like, and 'caring' was not one of his dad's qualities.

They entered the house and he reluctantly took the portable phone Aunt Karen lifted from the kitchen bench. He took a deep breath. "Hello?"

"Seb!" Dad's voice growled through the phone. "What's going on, boy?"

"Wh-what do you mean?" he stammered.

"I've been trying your mobile and it's not even ringing! I hope for dear sake you haven't lost it!"

"No, it's still fine," Seb answered, wincing.

"Well, where *is* it then? And why aren't you answering it?"

"It's switched off."

"Switched off! Haha! Don't you tell me you switched it off! It's never out of your hand!"

"Well," Seb took a deep breath, "I didn't exactly switch it off. Uncle Matt did."

"Matt! Why, the… if I get the hold of… what business is it of his… " Dad spluttered.

"He confiscated it!"

There was silence. Then, "He *what*?"

"He confiscated it," Seb repeated quietly.

"I heard you the first time," Dad blustered. "What I want to know is *why!*"

"Um, as a punishment… "

"For what?"

"I crashed his pickup truck." He waited for the explosion.

Suddenly, a burst of laughter rang through the phone. Seb pulled the phone away from his ear and stared at it.

"Ah-hahahahahaha! That's priceless! Oh, revenge is sweet! Serves the religious bigot right! I'm sure he was mad! Ah-hahahahaha!"

Seb shook his head. Who *was* this madman? He couldn't believe that he could be so bitter towards someone just because he was a Christian. And after all Matt had done for him! Dad was being unfair!

"Dad!"

The laughter subsided a little. "Yes, son?" he spluttered, through suppressed chortles. "I have to say, son, you've finally made me proud of you."

Proud! All these years without a word of praise from his dad and finally...

"Dad! I stole the truck and crashed it! That's nothing to be proud of! It's ruined and Uncle Matt can't afford to replace it."

"Hahaha! Even better!" laughed Dad again. "But tell me, son... was he mad? Did the holy roller lose his rag?"

"No, he didn't," replied Seb, getting angrier by the second. "He *forgave* me! And he has been nothing but kind to me and has taught me things and talked to me, and told me he was proud of me... for doing good stuff. And how *dare* you say those things?! You are a sorry excuse for a dad and I..." He stopped. Telling his dad he hated him could very well mean his death when he went home again. His dad in a drunken rage was uncontrollable.

"You what?" sneered Dad. "Were you going to say you hate me? Huh? Ah well, at least they haven't brainwashed you yet. Christians aren't supposed to hate people. Ha! Notice I said 'supposed'! Bunch of gullible hypocrites, the whole lot of them..."

Seb tuned him out. How had he ever wanted to make that man proud of him?

"And Seb?"

"Yes, Dad," Seb replied reluctantly.

"I was phoning to tell you not to be sucked into going to church with them tomorrow. That's the last place you want to be. Promise me you won't go."

"If they want me there, I'll go," he said.

"NO, YOU WON'T," his dad bellowed down the phone. "And if I hear you've become a Christian, I will personally…"

Uncle Matt came into the kitchen just then. "Is that your dad?" he asked softly.

Seb nodded.

Matt held out his hand for the phone and Seb gladly relinquished it.

Dad continued to rant about the consequences should Seb become a Christian. Matt waited patiently until Dad started running out of things to say.

"Well, Alan, how are you?" asked Matt.

The yelling started up again. Seb could almost hear every word. "…brainwashing my son…no God…hypocrites…"

"Alan! *Alan!*" called Matt firmly. The yelling finally sputtered to a stop. "I'm not listening to that. You know it's not true. I just want to say that your son is doing well here. He's a hard worker, he'll give anything a go and we're enjoying having him around. But you have to remember that he's old enough to make up his own mind about what you call 'religion'. You have given him your side. Don't you think it's time he heard the truth? Now," he continued, without giving Seb's dad a chance to answer, "we have work to do. Goodbye!" And with that, he pressed the 'End Call' button and set the handset on the bench.

Seb slumped against the bench. "Thanks, Uncle Matt," he said.

Matt smiled. "No bother, Seb!" he said. "I was in the office and I detected he was giving you a hard time. If he phones again, I'll ask Karen to pass the phone to me first."

Seb breathed a sigh of relief. He certainly didn't want to go through that again for a long time.

"I wonder why your dad is so bitter about anything to do with God and the Bible?" Uncle Matt mused. "He certainly has a vicious hatred of Christians. I can't help but think something has happened in his life to cause him to become like that."

Seb shrugged. He didn't know. To him, his dad had always detested religion. He'd always just assumed his dad had thought it through and come to a logical conclusion that there was no God. But it was pretty obvious now, that when it came to his dad, very few of his thoughts and actions were based on logic.

Seb sat with the McRoss family, Lavinia to one side and Martha on the other. He could see the Harveys across the aisle to his right, taking up two rows. Tommy and Madge were there, Madge dressed in a voluminous purple dress and hat and singing dreadfully off-key.

There were no stained-glass windows or oppressive dark corners; instead, light oak and cream painted walls gave the room a fresh, airy feel. Bible verses were on the walls, and behind the platform golden letters spelled out the words, 'CHRIST DIED FOR OUR SINS'. It was not at all how Seb had imagined 'church' to be.

The speaker for that evening was middle-aged and pleasant, and called the listeners 'my friends'. His text for that evening was what he called 'the best known verse in the Bible'. He quoted it often. "For God so loved the world that He gave His only begotten Son, that whoever believes in Him should not perish but have everlasting life."

Strange, thought Seb, *that almost sounds familiar.* He figured he must have seen it somewhere before. Maybe Matt and Karen wrote that verse on their Christmas card one year.

The preacher was speaking on each phrase of his text. " 'For God...'," he said. "The Bible begins with these words, 'In the beginning God created the heavens and the earth.' Before there were ever people, there was God. Before there was even a universe, there was God. He is eternal – He always existed. There was never a time when God wasn't there. Believing that there is a God is fundamental to all that follows in the rest of the verse, my friends."

Seb looked up at the man, narrowing his eyes slightly. Who had told him there would be an atheist in his congregation tonight? Well, maybe a questioning atheist, he conceded. But still an atheist. Even with all the evidence pointing to the existence of a Creator, he still wasn't yet fully convinced.

Seb was quiet in the jeep on the way home. He'd never heard

what Christians termed 'the gospel' before. He hadn't realised that a Christian wasn't just someone who believed that God existed, or who attended church. Instead, a Christian was actually someone who had realised that Jesus Christ, God's Son, had come to earth to die for their sins and rose again from the dead, and had trusted Him. Becoming a Christian was obviously a life-changing experience. Seb caught his lip between his teeth. Was brainwashing so effective that it could change the way people lived? And did atheism change people for the better? Maybe Mr Symons lived a good life, he really didn't know anything about him outside of school, but he certainly hadn't seen any evidence in his dad's life in any case.

Chapter Fourteen

Monday morning dawned bright and clear, exactly as the forecast had predicted. Aunt Karen had cooked up a large Ulster fry. It was going to be a busy few days and the silaging team needed all the energy they could get.

After the morning reading they made their way outside. Tommy had just arrived in his Massey Ferguson tractor. Uncle Matt gave everyone instructions on what they were to do.

"Joe, would you be happy enough buckraking for a while?"

Joe nodded. "No bother, Matt!"

"I'll drive the harvester, and the three of you," Matt continued, nodding towards Seb, Lavinia and Tommy, "can cart the grass to the silo. Seb, maybe for the first run, go with Vinnie, she'll give you a few tips and pointers so you'll know exactly what you're going to do. You'll do great." He smiled at Seb.

Seb straightened his shoulders and stood tall. What had he to be scared of? If Uncle Matt thought he could do it...

He followed Lavinia to the tractor parked across the yard. They'd already hitched the trailers on before breakfast that morning. She swung herself up and Seb clambered up after her. As they were waiting to follow Uncle Matt's harvester, Lavinia spoke to Seb. "Did you hear that one of the Harveys' neighbours had his cattle stolen last night?"

Seb's head turned sharply to look at her. "So they haven't given up, then?" he said. "How many did they take?"

"I think it was six this time. The man has quite a large beef farm."

"And I take it he heard nothing?"

"Not a thing," replied Lavinia. "Caleb has some beef cattle. Not many, but he has put a lot of work into them, and they are worth a lot. He's getting worried."

The harvester lumbered out of the shed. It was a huge green and white monster, with a large cylindrical metal attachment – the pickup reel, Lavinia called it – at the front, and a chute protruding from the top. It made its way slowly to the nearest field. Lavinia started her tractor and followed.

"Is he going to do anything about it?" Seb asked.

"Who, Caleb?"

"Yes."

"I don't think there's anything he can do, apart from house them in the shed. And that's not really an option with the cost of feed. He needs them to be grazing as much as possible during the summer."

"If we just knew when they were going to strike next and where…"

Lavinia laughed. "What would you do? I mean, there are obviously a number of them. You aren't going to be able to sort out three or four big strong men on your own!"

The harvester was stopped at the beginning of a row of grass, waiting for them to catch up. Lavinia pulled up alongside.

The harvester began to roar and the pickup reel began to turn. Lavinia pulled slightly ahead.

"Can you see where the grass is coming from?" she asked Seb, as she drove forwards.

Seb craned his neck to see behind him. "Yes, I see that," he said, watching the chute now angled towards Lavinia's trailer.

"Make sure you don't drive too close, or it'll go over the other side. Don't go too far away either, or it'll not go into the trailer at all. Same with how far you are in front of the harvester. You might need to go a bit further forward to fill the back part of the trailer towards the end, but Dad can change the direction of the chute anyway if he needs to."

Seb watched. It didn't seem too hard right now, but anything could happen.

When the trailer was full, Lavinia pulled away and headed back to the yard. Tommy, who had been driving behind, now pulled into position for the next load.

They made their way to the yard and Lavinia tipped the load of grass in the silo – a large three-sided concrete area, where Joe was waiting with another piece of machinery to push the grass into the silo and compress it into smaller bulk.

Lavinia drove away, the back door of the trailer banging as it settled back into position, small clumps of grass dislodging onto the ground.

She stopped beside the tractor Seb had learned to drive. "Have fun," she called, as he climbed down.

Pulling himself into the cab, he turned the key. The tractor roared to life. His hands shook slightly as he grasped the large steering wheel. He was actually going to help with silaging. It wasn't too long ago that he hadn't had a clue what silaging was, and had never even seen a tractor up close before.

He moved off towards the field, slowing to let Tommy, with his full load, exit first. Then he drove into position behind Lavinia.

It was soon time for Seb to take Lavinia's place. He drove into position and glanced back at Uncle Matt. He nodded and gave him the thumbs up. The chute began to blow the grass into his trailer. Seb tried to keep in a straight line, but it was harder than it looked, trying to keep an eye on the trailer at the same time. Once or twice the grass missed the trailer altogether and Seb groaned. He was a novice and it was obvious. Finally the trailer filled and a glance at Uncle Matt's thumb confirmed it was time to head for Joe.

Reversing and tipping the trailer took all Seb's skill. Glancing back he was concerned to see the pile had landed a little farther from the rest of the grass than he'd intended. A look at Joe's annoyed face through the cab of the JCB telehandler he was driving was not reassuring.

The morning passed in a blur of carting grass – field to silo and back. As they moved to more distant fields there was less time available between leaving to tip a load and being back, ready to get filled up again, so it took all of Seb's concentration to work efficiently. By the end of the morning he was driving in a much straighter line and tipping the grass closer to the silo.

He was ready for lunch when he saw Aunt Karen waving at him on the way back from the silo. They all got washed up and gathered round the table for big bowls of vegetable broth. A huge dish of peeled, boiled potatoes was in the centre of the table and everyone lifted one and set it into their broth. Seb had never heard of putting boiled potatoes into a bowl of soup, but he shrugged and figured he may as well join in. Everyone had a glass of milk. Seb wasn't too keen on the milk here – it tasted a lot different to the milk he was used to drinking, creamier and with a stronger taste, not that he drank much milk anyway. But he bravely swallowed it down.

After lunch, Uncle Matt pushed his chair back. "Right, people," he said, "time to get at the work again." Seb pulled his boots on again and headed across the yard to the tractor. He was next to collect the load, but Uncle Matt had only the first few metres lifted before the harvester began to make a terrible noise. Matt stopped the engine and climbed out.

After a few minutes of inspection he called to Seb. "Go and get Joe. I'll need his help to figure out what's going on."

Work was now at a standstill. It seemed that the good progress made in the morning was now being counteracted by a mechanical problem. After checking the huge machine, the diagnosis was made and Joe was despatched to the agricultural dealers for the appropriate bearing replacement.

"Seb, why don't you go with him?" Uncle Matt asked. "You might as well head out for the run. Nothing's happening here."

Seb got into the passenger seat of Matt's jeep and they set off towards town. Joe wasn't as careful a driver as Matt and tended to swing out of road ends without stopping. He drove fast and sloppily.

As they drove past Barry's dealership he could see the Ranger back on display. He was surprised. He'd assumed that the cattle rustlers used it every time, but maybe after what had happened to the wing mirror...

"Nice truck, that Ranger," commented Joe.

Seb absently agreed. He was stumped. His theory about the rustlers using the Ranger had been blown apart. It was time for a trip to the latest crime scene.

Fixing the bearing on the harvester took all afternoon. Seb and Lavinia started the milking while Matt and Joe worked on the harvester.

"The Ranger is sitting on display at Barry's," Seb told her while wiping down the cows' udders.

Lavinia gave him a quizzical look. "Is that strange?" she asked. "It just must mean he's got it fixed."

"But you said Caleb's neighbour had cattle stolen last night."

Lavinia turned to look at him, the stainless steel clusters of the milking machine spread between her fingers. "I'd forgotten about your theory," she said. "Maybe Barry got it cleaned up earlier this time."

"I don't think that's possible," Seb answered. "To get it back in showroom condition takes a lot of work and there was never any sign of anyone else apart from Barry when we were there."

Lavinia shrugged. "Maybe he has had enough with them damaging the wing mirror," she suggested.

"That's what I wondered," said Seb thoughtfully. "But maybe he knew we were on to him."

"I wonder what they're using now," said Lavinia.

"Vinnie..." Seb began.

Lavinia shook her head. "No, Seb!"

"What do you mean? I haven't asked anything yet!"

"You want to go prowling around Barry's yard again. Don't you?"

Seb shook his head. "No, not that. But do you think we could visit Caleb's neighbour? Maybe they've left some more vital evidence!"

As it turned out, there was no time for going anywhere that night. The breakdown had meant that they'd lost half a day and they had to work late to make up for lost time.

Seb fell into bed exhausted. His muscles ached and his eyelids drooped. There were many acres of silage left to bring in. It would be a while before they would be free to search for anything that would give them a clue as to who was spiriting the cattle across the border in the small hours of the night.

Chapter Fifteen

Seb had never worked so hard in his entire life. Each night when he collapsed into bed he could still hear the roar of the machinery and smell the freshly cut grass. He even awoke in the small hours to find himself sitting up in bed, looking over one shoulder, hands clutching an imaginary steering wheel.

But in a few days it was over. The fields lay bare, shaved to golden stubble. Joe left after morning milking each day to help another farmer with his silage, and Lavinia spent part of each day leading her heifer around the yard.

Then came the phone call which shattered the idyllic world and pulled Seb back to reality. Gran was dead.

Dressed in his best clothes, Seb sat in the back seat of Uncle Matt's jeep on their way to Gran's funeral. Lavinia and Martha were spending the day with the Harveys. Seb's knees started to tremble as he recognised the familiar skyline ahead. The buildings condensed and grew, the traffic became more intense and the noise louder. Seb's heart began to thump, an off-beat rhythm to his trembling knees. Aunt Karen leaned around to smile at Seb. "Doing okay back there?" she asked.

Seb nodded.

"Bit nervous?"

Seb nodded again. The last time he'd spoken with his dad he'd almost told him he hated him. The closer they got to Belfast, the more his courage receded. He wasn't looking forward to seeing his dad again. He hoped Uncle Matt and Aunt Karen would be close by.

The funeral was held in a funeral parlour. Gran had grown up going to church, but hadn't attended in years. Going to a funeral parlour sat better with Dad too; Seb didn't think Dad would be able to walk into a church building without feeling a compulsion to cause destruction, so great was his hatred.

Gran had requested that a minister conduct the service, Seb learned, as they walked through the glass doors into the lobby, where Mum and Dad greeted those who had come to pay their condolences.

Mum looked small and fragile beside Dad, her shoulders hunched, heavy makeup unable to hide the wrinkles and worry lines. Her hair looked brassy and frizzy and her black suit had seen better days. She looked up. A tentative smile crossed her face. Aunt Karen nudged Seb across. "Go over and speak to them," she whispered. "We'll be right here."

As Seb approached, Mum came to meet him. "You look great," she whispered, as she gave him a hug. "The country really agrees with you."

"So, here's the smarty pants who has gone all religious on us!" Dad's voice boomed across the hushed silence.

Seb could feel his resentment rising.

"Now, Alan," whispered Mum. "This isn't the time or the place."

Dad opened his mouth, then shut it as another cluster of mourners entered the lobby. When they had shaken hands with Dad and Mum, Matt and Karen moved across to speak to them.

Karen whispered something to Seb's mum as she gave her a tight hug. Mum nodded, then wiped her eyes with a tissue she pulled from her jacket pocket.

As Seb watched from the sidelines, he could hardly believe his eyes. Uncle Matt was standing, his hand outstretched for Dad to shake. Dad was looking at it as if it was a poisonous snake, a look of utter revulsion on his face. His eyes moved upwards to Matt's face and he shook his head, lips pursed together, eyes narrowed. Then he turned away.

Seb looked into the open coffin. The black hair stood in harsh contrast to her waxy face. It was hard to imagine her as the Gran he knew, yet there were enough familiar features to recognise her. The large, hooked nose, the close-set eyes, even the wrinkles around her mouth from years of pursing her lips around her beloved cigarettes.

He suddenly remembered the cigarette packet. *Smoking kills.*

Death is not the end, came the voice. As he looked at Gran's lifeless body, he wondered. Could life just drain from someone, and that was the end? Or was it perhaps as he had heard on Sunday - that the soul will live on forever, even when the body is dead? As he stood there, imagining what it would be like to face death, he knew one thing for sure. When that moment came, it would be too late to find out that the Bible was right after all.

After a reading of the 23rd Psalm, the minister made no further reference to the Bible. "Well, everyone, Dorothy's family and friends, we are here to celebrate Dorothy's life. This could be a sad day, but we'll choose to focus on the good memories and celebrate the times we shared with her. Dorothy had many interests. She loved her family – her son, Alan, daughter-in-law, Julie, and her grandson, Sebastian."

Seb cringed. No one called him Sebastian. And he certainly hadn't seen much evidence of her love. He thought back to the last time he saw her. His last memory of his grandmother. Black hair on end, shaking a fist, raging at him for stealing her cigarettes. It wasn't exactly the warm, cosy family picture the minister was painting.

"Dorothy also loved her bingo. Every day she faithfully went down to the wee bingo club. She was always in her element at bingo. After her family, bingo was what she lived and breathed... "

Seb listened to the minister prattling on. He shared the odd joke and funny story, and the 'mourners' politely chuckled. Seb couldn't help but feel that if bingo was all there was to Gran's life, it was quite pointless. She'd made a few friends, played a lot of bingo and likely single-handedly kept the tobacco industry afloat. Was that all? At the end, was this really all that mattered? Surely there was more to life than just doing what you wanted? Yet this was atheism's message. Like the advertisement on the London buses a few years back – *There's probably no God, now stop worrying and enjoy your life.* He wasn't sure if his gran had believed in the existence of God or not; she certainly hadn't given Him much thought if she had. But Seb's dad certainly didn't believe in God. But he seemed to worry a lot, and, try as he might, he certainly didn't seem to be enjoying life at all. Now, Uncle Matt and Aunt Karen, on the other hand, who did believe in God, appeared to worry less than anyone he knew *and* appeared to be enjoying life to the fullest. He could almost imagine that he could believe in the existence of God, but there was something, he didn't know what exactly, that was holding him back.

After the funeral everyone went to a nearby hotel for a light lunch. As Seb sat with his plate of sandwiches and sausage rolls, his mum pulled a chair out from beside him and sat down. Dad was nowhere to be seen.

She put a hand on his arm. "Tell me, Seb," she asked quietly. "How are you getting on at the farm?"

Seb nodded. "Okay," he answered.

"What sort of things are you doing?"

"Milking, clearing out calf houses, driving tractors..."

"Really?!" she exclaimed. "They're letting you do that?"

Seb nodded, peeling open the finger sandwich to inspect the contents. Something pale and mushy. He sniffed it. Fish. He set it back on his plate.

Mum bit her lip. "Your dad said something about crashing Matt's pickup truck..." Her eyes pleaded with Seb to tell her it was all an exaggeration.

Seb looked down.

"Did you?" she pressed.

Seb nodded.

"Oh, Seb," Mum groaned. "How badly did you crash it?"

"I rolled it," he muttered.

Mum grabbed his chin and lifted his head. "Seb!" she hissed, alarmed. "Were you hurt?"

Seb shook his head.

"Well, that's good. But can it be fixed?"

Seb shook his head again.

Mum's shoulders slumped and she put her head in her hands. "Where did I go wrong?" she groaned.

At that moment Uncle Matt and Aunt Karen joined them, sitting opposite. Mum raised her head to look at Matt.

"Matt..." she began.

"Don't worry about it, Julie," Matt said, smiling. "I can guess what you've just discovered. I didn't want to give you anything to worry about. Seb has apologised, I've forgiven him, and that's all there is to it. Apart from having his smartphone confiscated, but we keep him so busy I don't think he misses it anymore!"

Uncle Matt was right. Seb hadn't thought about his phone in days.

His mum looked unconvinced. "But, Matt, we need to help you out. You lost a lot of money."

"Julie," Matt shook his head firmly, "just forget it! None of you owe us a thing. We said we'd treat Seb like our own, and we're sticking to that."

Mum's eyes welled up with tears and she reached across the table to Matt and Karen, squeezing their hands. "Thank you so much!"

"Well, now, this is a cosy little scene of family love," came a voice. Seb's dad strode into the room, a large glass filled with a brownish brew in his hand. He set it on the table and threw himself onto the chair beside Mum. He put his arm around her and squeezed her shoulder. "Don't you be getting yourself all *saved*, talking to these Bible bashers," he sneered. Mum squirmed away from his painful grasp. "What's wrong, don't like showing a bit of affection in public?" he laughed, taking a swig from his glass.

Seb cringed. He had almost forgotten how mean his dad could be when he drank. He could feel himself retreating into the inner part of his being, bottling up his feelings and screwing the lid on tight.

Uncle Matt caught his eye across the table. "Ready to go?" he mouthed.

Seb nodded.

As they stood up to leave, Seb looked into his mum's eyes. He could see the fear and dejection. They both knew what was ahead for her that evening. Not only did the alcohol bring out the monster in Seb's dad, but now it would be aggravated by being exposed to the light of true life and godly love evident in the couple who were even now making a final attempt to reach out to him, despite his evident hatred of them.

Chapter Sixteen

Seb sat on the back doorstep rubbing Jess's ears. She pressed against him and licked his arm. Her belly was large and swollen; the pups were due any day now.

He couldn't help but think of the previous day's events and the contrast between his home and family in Belfast and the home here. Could something as simple as a belief in God make all the difference? He knew people who believed in a god of some sort, people like his next-door neighbours in Belfast, the Peters. Whatever sort of god they believed in didn't affect their lives – they smoke, drank, swore, fought, and weren't a whole lot different from Dad. But their god didn't seem to be the God Matt and Karen believed in. Or maybe those people weren't true Christians after all, ones who had trusted in Christ, as the preacher had said last Sunday.

He wished he could know for sure that there was a God. Yes, the evidence seemed to be convincing. He wasn't happy anymore with his teachers' explanation for the beginning of the universe, or the theory of evolution. He could see the amazing design in the creatures around him – the way the cows were able to turn grass into milk, the way Jess was carrying a number of little pups, who didn't even exist a few months ago. Even his own human body, each part and system functioning perfectly.

Evolution couldn't adequately explain how all the organs, systems, cells and DNA came into being and worked amazingly, and it certainly couldn't explain how humans could differentiate between right and wrong. Who told people that certain things were wrong? And how can anything be wrong if we are all just what Mr Symons called 'matter' - products of a chance happening?

Seb shook his head. It didn't make any sense.

The back door opened and Uncle Matt stepped out. He lowered himself onto the step beside Seb, but said nothing. Jess stretched onto her side and Seb softly rubbed her large belly.

"Uncle Matt?" he asked.

"Yes, Seb?"

Seb cleared his throat. He wasn't sure how to ask the question uppermost in his mind. "How..." he began. He cleared his throat. "How can you know... for sure... that there is a God?" he finished in a rush.

Matt smiled thoughtfully. "You mean is there any way that we can know, beyond any doubt whatsoever? Apart from all the evidence that we see around us, and all the other ways we've discussed lately?"

Seb nodded. People tried to explain away what Uncle Matt called 'evidence'. Atheists denied God's existence because they couldn't physically see Him. How could someone know for sure?

"You know," Uncle Matt continued, "I believe that God has given us all the evidence we need. It's typical of human nature, that no matter how much evidence God gives us, we always want more. And if God were to give us what we feel would completely convince us, we still wouldn't believe!"

Seb frowned. He wasn't sure about that.

"God sent His Son, the Lord Jesus Christ, from heaven. He was God, but He came to earth as a human being. He was born in Bethlehem and grew up in the village of Nazareth. People saw Him, talked with Him and watched what He did. He was completely sinless – perfect in every way. And He worked many miracles – He healed the sick, made blind people to see and deaf people to hear. He even brought dead people back to life. He multiplied bread and fish; He calmed storms just by speaking. But they crucified Him. And do you know what they said to Him as He was hanging on that cross? They said, 'Let the Christ, the King of Israel, descend now from the cross, that we may see and believe.' Do you think that the One Who could raise the dead could come down from a cross?"

Seb shrugged. "I suppose so," he replied.

"So why hadn't they already believed? Do you think if He had done what they'd asked that it would actually have caused them to believe?"

Seb thought about it. He supposed not.

"You know, Seb, at the end of it all, to believe or not believe is a choice. God has given you more than enough evidence for you to believe in His existence. You can believe what the evidence is clearly pointing to, or you can refuse to believe it and continue to tell yourself there is no God."

So it was a decision at the end of the day. He had seen the evidence – in creation, in moral order, even in the lives of his uncle and aunt. He just had to let himself believe what the evidence was pointing to. And the evidence was clear and inarguable. For the first time, Seb could say without doubt: *There is a God.*

Jess lay on the sawdust under the warm infrared lamp, seven little smooth black and white bundles lined up, pink mouths to Jess's belly. Seb looked over the partition at the cosy sight. Seeing the pups being born was one of the best sights he'd ever witnessed. Each little parcel being released from the birth sac, cleaned and separated from the placenta by the capable mother herself, then nudged to the warm supply of milk. He was blown away by her God-given instinct. No one had ever taught Jess what to do, yet she birthed her pups like a pro!

The last one had been a lot smaller; the runt, Uncle Matt said. From what Seb could see, this one looked like a miniature Jess, with the same white stripe across the shoulders and a white front left paw.

Jess was looking quite exhausted. She raised her head to regard Seb with tired eyes, then bent down to lick the pup nearest her head. It wriggled, squeaked in complaint and went back to feeding. Seb smiled. He was looking forward to watching these little guys grow!

Uncle Matt dropped the rolled up paper and the jeep keys on the table before lunch on Wednesday. "Freddy Robertson lost four head of cattle last night," he said. "Sadie down at the shop was saying."

Seb looked up, holding the cutlery Aunt Karen had asked him to arrange around the table. "Does he live near here?" he asked.

"About a mile or so on up the road. It's worrying, this spate of rustling. And no one seems to have a clue who it is that's doing it."

Seb didn't say anything. He didn't think Uncle Matt would take him seriously if he suggested that Barry was responsible.

Lavinia spent most of the day doing some last minute practice for the show, so it wasn't until after dinner that Seb managed to get speaking to her on her own as they walked down the back lane.

"Did you hear there have been more cattle stolen?" Seb said, pulling a long piece of grass from the hedge and shredding it as they walked.

"No, whose were they?"

"Freddy somebody."

"Freddy Robertson?"

Seb nodded. "Yes, I think that was the name."

"The rotters!" she exclaimed, her lips curling up in disgust. "I can't believe they keep getting away with it!"

"Me neither," said Seb. They had reached the field where the cows were. The cow nearest to them regarded them lazily, chewing her cud, her side giving the occasional tremor to dislodge the buzzing flies.

"Vinnie, I wonder is there any pattern to these rustlings?"

"I don't know, Seb, I never thought to take a note," Lavinia replied.

"Well, Tommy's were stolen a couple of nights after I arrived, so that was a Wednesday night, and the Harveys' neighbour had his stolen last Sunday night. Last night was Tuesday night." Seb scratched his head.

"And don't forget Bobby Davison. His were stolen before Tommy's, maybe on a Monday night."

They were silent a moment.

"I'm not seeing a pattern. Are you?" Seb asked.

Lavinia shook her head. "Monday, Wednesday, Sunday, then nothing for a week, then Tuesday. I don't see any pattern at all."

"Unless there were others we don't know about, maybe in other areas?"

Lavinia shrugged. "I think we'd have heard," she said. "People come to Harvey's store from all around, and farmers like to talk. Caleb would have said."

Seb grinned. "Really?" he teased. "You must be in contact with him more than you let on!"

Lavinia jabbed her elbow in his ribs. "Shut up, Seb!" she said, going red. "We have to take the heifer to the show tomorrow afternoon," she continued, changing the subject. "The dairy judging starts early on Friday."

"Is she ready, do you think?" Seb asked.

She shrugged. "I hope so, but she's unpredictable, so you never know."

"I've never been to the show before," admitted Seb.

"You haven't?" asked Lavinia, then she gave a chuckle. "Well, I suppose why would you go to an agricultural show, after all? It's not really something that most city boys would find good fun. All those animals, machinery, Women's Institute competitions, cookery demonstrations... Oh, there's usually a display of some sort as well, maybe motocross or something like that."

Seb was intrigued. It sounded like an unusual combination to him. "Do many people go?"

"Oh, yes!" Lavinia laughed. "They come from all over the country. There are loads of smaller, local shows, but this is the biggest one here. I've been going since I was a baby. I wouldn't miss it."

Lavinia's enthusiasm was contagious. Seb found himself looking forward to the show, and being amongst farmers for the day. He laughed.

Lavinia looked at him quizzically. "What's so funny?" she asked.

"Just thinking it's ironic that the city boy is looking forward to the *agricultural* show!" he replied.

Lavinia smiled. "Well, I don't know who that bristly, cross Seb was, who arrived here at the beginning of the summer, but I'm very glad he's gone. I like this Seb much better!"

Seb looked away, embarrassed. He never thought that his chattery, know-it-all cousin would turn out to be so great either, but he certainly wasn't going to go all mushy about it!

Chapter Seventeen

A breeze blowing through both open doorways wafted the strong bovine smell, mingled with fresh straw and shampoo, around the large shed housing the dairy cattle. A cacophony of bellows and lows mingled with the relaxed conversations of the owners. Seb had never realised there were so many different breeds of cattle. He looked down the row to where reddish-brown and white cattle were tied to the railing. Beyond those were small, pale brown cattle, soft eyes rimmed dark, as if they were wearing eyeliner.

"Jerseys," explained Lavinia, following his gaze. "Pretty cattle, but very strong. Not as good-tempered as our girls." She patted her heifer's rump. The heifer shifted her feet on the fresh straw.

"And those brown and white ones?" asked Seb.

"Ayrshires," Lavinia explained. "A few farmers have whole herds of Ayrshires, but the majority of dairy cattle around these parts are Holsteins."

"Is there a shed for the beef cattle?" Seb asked.

"Yes," Lavinia brushed her hands on her legs. "Would you like to see them?"

Seb nodded. Why not?

He followed Lavinia into another shed. This one was even bigger and noisier, with all colours of cattle. They began to meander through the aisles. All shapes and sizes seemed to be present. Seb took a step away from a particularly large, white bull. He had been washed and brushed, and his hair looked soft and gently curled. Along the next aisle stood a black cow, tiny calf at her feet. The calf cocked his head to look curiously at Seb, large ears at attention. He stuck his wet, black nose in the air and opened his mouth. *Baawww!* Seb smiled.

Lavinia gave a running commentary on all the breeds they walked past. Seb knew he'd never remember even half of the names. *Charolais*; the white bull. *Limousins*; a deep auburny-red. *Herefords*; reddish-brown bodies and ears with white bellies and faces. *Aberdeen Angus*; pure black cattle.

"What breed of cattle does Caleb have?" Seb asked.

"He has a mixture of Limousins crossed with Angus," she answered. "Most beef farmers don't have pure-bred cattle. By crossing two breeds you can get good traits from both breeds. For example, maybe one is a good breed for weight gain, but isn't so good at calving, so you cross with a different breed which is known for ease of calving."

Seb nodded. It made sense. But he still had so much to learn.

They walked back to the dairy shed. Uncle Matt, Lavinia and Seb had brought the heifer to the show that afternoon so she would be well settled before the judging on Friday. An old university acquaintance of Matt's, Laura Sommerville, had a number of cows tied beside Lavinia's heifer. Laura and her husband were planning to stay there that night with their own cows. Uncle Matt had arranged for Laura to keep an eye on Lavinia's heifer as well.

"I don't know why we just can't stay all night," complained Lavinia.

"Vinnie, I told you," her dad answered as they walked back to the jeep, "cattle sheds at shows are no place for a teenage girl at night. I used to show cattle for a farmer back when I was at uni, and I don't want you in the middle of all the drinking that goes on when the visitors leave."

Lavinia looked unconvinced, but her dad wasn't going to budge.

Seb leaned on the wooden fence of the enclosure and watched the black and white cattle being led around the ring by their white-clad handlers. Lavinia's face was a study in determined concentration.

"The heifer's walking well," Uncle Matt commented from beside Seb.

"Vinnie's been working hard lately," Seb replied.

Uncle Matt nodded. "Takes her a while to get going sometimes, but when she finally begins, she gives it her best."

The judge, an older gentleman dressed in a tweed jacket and holding a wooden walking stick, seriously regarded the competing animals.

"He's an old-school judge," said Matt. "He's from the south of England and knows Holsteins inside out. Whoever gets first place will deserve to win."

"What is he looking for?" asked Seb.

"Quite a lot of things," laughed Uncle Matt. "He's looking at the general appearance, making sure she's in proportion, straight back, deep chest, wide ribs..."

The judge appeared to look down. "He'll be checking their movement, making sure they have a good, straight stride and the feet are pointing in the right direction."

The handlers began to guide the heifers to stand in a row. Suddenly, Lavinia's heifer stopped dead. She tugged at the halter, leaning back to pull the heifer forwards, but she wouldn't budge.

"Push her back," muttered Matt.

As if she had heard her dad, Lavinia pushed. The heifer's head went to one side and she began to move again, albeit in a different direction. Lavinia took advantage of the momentum and quickly guided her into position.

"Good girl," said Matt softly.

Seb watched as Lavinia looked down at the heifer's feet and then proceeded to rest the toe of her boot on the back left hoof. The heifer pulled her foot away from the pressure and set it back down. Still not happy, Lavinia repeated the process until the hoof was placed in the correct position.

The judge was now standing behind the animals, his bushy grey eyebrows lowered in concentration.

"He's inspecting the rump and placement of the back legs," Matt explained. "The legs should be straight, not bowed."

"How do you think Vinnie's heifer will do?" asked Seb.

Uncle Matt nodded. "I think she'll do well," he replied. "That's a fantastic heifer there," he pointed to the animal at the end of the line, "but Vinnie's isn't far off."

Uncle Matt's predictions were right. Lavinia shook hands with the judge and accepted the blue second place rosette. She smiled at her dad and Seb and gave them the thumbs up.

After the photographs had been taken, Lavinia led her heifer out of the ring and back to the shed.

"I'm pleased with that," she told her dad and Seb, as she tied the animal to the bar. "A first would have been amazing, but second is the next best thing!" She giggled at her obvious statement.

"I think this girl has the makings of a really good cow," said Matt. "Give her a couple of years and she'll maybe make a first then."

Lavinia smiled, and looked proudly at her heifer. Her stomach growled and she giggled again. "I'm starving!" she exclaimed. "Can we go and find something to eat?"

Uncle Matt looked at his watch. "Sure, no problem," he said. "Your mum and Martha should be here shortly. I'll wait for them here. You have your phone?"

Lavinia patted her pocket and nodded.

"Okay, I'll phone you when we're leaving. Oh, and here…" he called, holding out a couple of notes, "this is for your lunch and whatever else you see that you'd like."

Seb's eyes opened wide. That was enough to buy them a few lunches!

"Thanks, Dad," Lavinia called as they set off.

"This is good," Seb mumbled, around a huge bite of a pork and stuffing roll.

"I know," Lavinia answered. "I get this every year. It's one of the things I look forward to about the show."

They were seated at a picnic table near the burger vans and food stalls. Most people hadn't thought about lunch yet, so there had been no queue for the food, and they had plenty of tables to choose from. It had turned out to be a warm day, and the crowds seemed to be increasing by the minute. Old men, dressed in their best jackets and tweed caps; young families, children riding on their fathers' shoulders; groups of young people, laughing and talking noisily: the whole spectrum of ages was present. They could hear the sizzle of the burgers from the nearby burger vans and in the distance the deep voice of a commentator echoing through the loudspeaker at the horse arena.

"That looks good," came a familiar voice.

Seb looked up. "Hi, Joe!"

Lavinia swallowed her bite and took a drink of orange Fanta. "It's amazing!" she exclaimed.

Joe laughed. "I'm sure it is, but I'd rather have a real burger! How did the heifer do?"

"Great! Second place!"

"Hey, congratulations!" said Joe. "I thought she was a good one. Better go and see what's to see. Talk to you later!"

"Is Joe here by himself?" Seb asked.

Lavinia shrugged. "I wouldn't think so," she replied. "He always has a lot of friends and, like, *hundreds* of cousins, and he seems to know everybody."

Seb finished his pork roll and crumpled his napkin. Lavinia swallowed her last bite and stood up. "Right, let's go! There're loads of interesting things here!"

They wandered around machinery stands, taking in the tractors, harvesters, telehandlers, diggers and other powerful-looking machines which Seb had no clue about. They looked at concrete products and gates and cattle crushes. They pressed through the crowds thronging the food tent and managed to find free samples of ice-cream, bread and strawberries. They even took in a cookery demonstration, although Seb wandered off halfway through, bored with the technical description of how to work marinade into chicken thighs. He returned in time to taste the results.

"Did you get the recipe?" he asked Lavinia as they walked away.

"Of course I did," she said. "It's actually really easy to make. We'll have to try it some night."

"Does Caleb like chicken with... What's it called?" He grabbed the page with the recipe. "Ginger and lime chicken on a bed of vermicelli noodles," he read.

Lavinia suddenly grabbed the page from him. "Keep your mouth *shut*," she hissed.

Seb laughed as he spotted Caleb coming towards them.

"Hi, Caleb," said Lavinia, brightly.

"Hi, Vinnie. Hi, Seb," replied Caleb.

"Vinnie was just wondering if you like ginger chicken and lime on a..."

Lavinia dug her elbow in his ribs.

"Ow! Is that not what it's called?"

Lavinia responded by standing on his toe.

Caleb watched the exchange with a bemused smile. "How did the heifer do?" he asked.

Lavinia shot one final warning glare at Seb before answering.

Five minutes later Lavinia looked around to see that her cousin had disappeared. She groaned. "We'll never find him here," she said.

"Sure we could phone him," Caleb suggested.

Lavinia shook her head. "He had his phone confiscated just after he arrived. He was supposed to stay with me all day."

"I'm sure we'll bump into him sooner or later," Caleb reassured her. "I mean, he can't exactly go anywhere outside of the showgrounds."

Lavinia nodded. "I suppose you're right," she said. "But maybe we should keep an eye out for him."

Seb perused the various stands. All manner of goods were on display, from massage chairs, to jewellery, to collars for dogs. People were trying to sell insurance, offer free assessments on electricity costs, and promote weekend breaks.

He made his way back outside. He'd exited through a different door and had ended up in the middle of equestrian stands, with clothing, saddles, blankets and boots. Horses didn't hold much interest for him, so he made his way to a lorry trailer set up as a stage with some loud country music pumping from the speakers. A live radio broadcast seemed to be in progress. He sat on the grass off to one side, his back to a white tent.

As he listened to the music, interspersed with commentary from the presenter, he gradually became aware of the sounds coming from inside the tent. He could hear the clink of bottles and laughter. *This must be the beer tent*, he thought to himself. A cluster of voices grew closer, so close, in fact, that it seemed they were sitting right next to Seb. They must be just on the other side of the canvas.

"That was a great night we had the other night!"

"What? Oh aye, at Downey's! I thought the big lad was going to have a fight on his hands with those two women after him!"

Raucous laughter followed.

"Hey, I didn't see any of you having women fighting over you," another deeper voice retorted.

"Aye, but did you see them? Faces like horses, the pair of them!"

"Steady on, man! Sure the big lad likes horses!"

More laughter.

The conversation continued in a similar vein for some minutes. Another loud country song from the cowboy hatted figure on the stage distracted Seb. He couldn't help his foot tapping the ground in time to the music. As the applause died away he turned his attention back to the conversation behind him in the tent.

"Those were quare beese we got the other night!"

Seb narrowed his eyes. He'd have to ask Lavinia what 'quare beese' were.

"Aye, he raises them well, that wee man. Worth going back for another look."

"Naw, it's too soon. Better wait a week or two."

"Well, any other potential candidates you've spotted?"

"Aye, I've the next ones looked out. You know Harvey's?"

Seb's ears pricked at the mention of Harvey's. Could it be the same Harvey's he knew?

"Aye, the supplier?"

"That's the one. Well, his wee lad has some fine stock. Worth taking a wee look at them."

Stock? Of what? Could it be they were talking about Caleb's cattle?

"Well, we'll get that organised. Speak to the Chief and see if that'll work. Any night not suit anybody?"

A chorus of grunts sounded. "Only night don't suit me is Saturday," said one individual. "I've other fish to fry!" That voice sounded very familiar...

"No bother, we'll avoid Saturday nights if we can. Would Monday night suit you all?"

Once again, a chorus of grunts.

What were these people planning? Wouldn't Caleb need to know if they were coming to look at his stock? And surely he would take them to the market if he wanted to sell them.

He could hear the chairs being pushed back from the table and the voices beginning to fade.

Seb suddenly sat bolt upright. They weren't men who bought cattle at all.

He had just overheard the planning meeting of the cattle rustlers.

And Caleb's cattle were next!

Chapter Eighteen

Seb jumped to his feet and began to run around the outside of the tent. He needed to get a look at these people. He ran around an affectionate couple locked in a passionate embrace, dodged a pram and jumped over a small dog. As he rounded the corner, he glanced to the left to check the way was clear… and caught his foot on a gigantic purple leg. As he lay sprawled on the gravel, he looked up in horror to see the waving green arms of the stilt walker vainly trying to regain balance, before he crashed to the ground on top of Seb.

"Seb! SEB!" Lavinia's voice registered on Seb's stunned brain. The stilt walker was trying to untangle himself from Seb as she came rushing over with Caleb close behind. Pushing her way through the growing crowd, she knelt beside him.

"Are you okay?" she asked.

"I think so," he answered, rubbing his shoulder where the giant's weight had mostly landed.

The tall man sat beside Seb on the ground. "What on earth were you trying to do, running around like that without looking where you were going?" he asked, angrily.

Seb saw red. "What were *you* doing so close to the edge of the tent?"

Two security guards came rushing over. "What's going on here?" the short, round one asked, his moustache bobbing as he spoke.

The stilt walker pointed at Seb. "He ran straight into me and knocked me down," he accused.

"Well, he was walking too close to the corner," Seb countered.

The female security guard looked at them both and pulled out her radio to call for medical assistance. Seb looked around and groaned. The men would be long gone by now. The frustration of losing track of the cattle rustlers was greater than the ache in his shoulder.

An hour later Seb left the first aid area, having had his shoulder examined by a doctor. He had been told it would likely be sore for a day or two, but would heal. The stilt walker had suffered nothing except a grazed elbow and wounded pride, despite falling from his great height.

"What *were* you doing, not looking where you were going?" Lavinia asked as they made their way back into the crowds.

"Yes, a gigantic green and purple man isn't exactly something you trip over without seeing!" laughed Caleb.

Seb shrugged, then clutched his shoulder at the pain the movement generated. "I was in a rush," he said. "I need to talk to you, Caleb."

Caleb's head swung around to look at Seb. He'd never heard him speak in such a sober, urgent tone.

"What is it?" asked Lavinia.

Seb shook his head. "We'd better go somewhere less noisy. And where there are less people."

Lavinia looked at her pale blue watch. "It's about half an hour until the stunt show begins," she said. "We could get something to eat and take it to the grandstand. There should be a fairly quiet corner there for a wee while."

Lavinia's idea of something to eat included candyfloss, fudge and chocolate from one of the Kearney's Sweet Treats stands dotted around the showgrounds. Caleb managed to buy crisps and bottles of Coke from a nearby ice-cream van and they made their way to the top of the stands with their unhealthy picnic.

Lavinia tore into the candyfloss. "Mmm, I love this stuff," she said around a large mouthful. She offered the bag to Seb and Caleb and they pulled off a large wisp each.

"Now, what were you saying, Seb?" Caleb asked.

Seb recounted how he had become aware of a conversation coming from the beer tent. "They were talking about something like 'square bees'," he said.

"Square bees?" Lavinia looked at Caleb, puzzled. He shrugged.

"Maybe it was a code name for cows," Seb continued, seeing the blank looks on his friends' faces. "Anyway, what they went on to say was…"

"Oh! I know!" Lavinia interrupted. "The word 'beese' can be used for cattle – with a hissing s, rather than a z sound. And 'quare' means 'good'. So they were talking about good cattle."

Seb sighed. They really did speak a different language in the country!

"Go on, Seb," said Caleb. "What else did they say?"

"They said that the last cattle they got were 'quare beese' and they wondered about going back for another look. I think they said that the wee man reared them well."

"Who was that?" asked Lavinia, reaching for another handful of candyfloss.

"I think I know now, but we'll see if you think the same at the end. Anyway, they wondered about any other possibilities… no, I think 'potential candidates' were the words they used. And someone mentioned Harvey's."

"What?" Caleb lifted an eyebrow. "Us?"

Seb continued. "They said that the 'wee lad'… I assume that must be you, Caleb," he nodded towards the wide eyed boy sitting on the other side of Lavinia, "has some fine stock and they were going to take a look."

"But why, Seb?" asked Caleb. "Do they want to buy them? Or do you think…" Suddenly he sat bolt upright as the realisation dawned on him. "The rustlers! The 'wee man' must be Freddy Robertson – they took his cattle on Tuesday night."

Lavinia swung around to look at Seb. "Is that who they were? What else did they say?" she asked urgently.

"They discussed which night would suit, and mentioned 'the Chief' – he must be the ringleader."

"And which night did they decide on?"

"Monday night," replied Seb. He counted on his fingers. "We have three days to come up with a plan."

"So that's why you were running? To see them?"

Seb nodded. "I can't believe I missed them. I was so close."

Crowds were beginning to fill the grandstand. The famous motocross rider and stuntman, Davy Highland, was due in the arena any minute. Except the showjumping was running over time as usual!

A group of raucous young men squeezed past Seb, Lavinia and Caleb to sit along the back row. "We'll talk about this later," Caleb said.

Despite the thoughts and plans going through his head, Seb enjoyed the show. The riders handled their bikes with skill, doing wheelies and jumps, then moving on to more dangerous tricks.

"Wow!" said Lavinia, as Davy himself let go of his bike completely mid-air, before grabbing it again with one hand and landing sitting perfectly balanced on the seat. The breeze carried the scent of petrol fumes towards the grandstand, and the air was filled with the revving of the bikes. It had an adrenaline-producing effect on Seb, and by the time the riders rode around the arena, waving goodbye to the crowd, Seb felt he could take on a whole team of rustlers single-handedly.

Lavinia's mobile phone blared out a catchy tune that Seb thought he recognised from the live radio show earlier, but she answered it before he managed to think of the words.

"Hi, Dad!...We're just leaving the grandstand – we were watching the Davy Highland show... Yes, it was good... Mmm, I think I'd like to stay on... Okay, he's here, I'll ask him... " She lifted her phone from her ear and turned to Seb. "Dad wants to know if you're ready to leave. He's heading back to do the milking, so you can go back with him to help if you like."

Seb nodded. "Yes, that's fine," he answered. He'd likely seen everything at the show anyway.

Lavinia spoke again to her dad, then ended the call. "You're to go back to the dairy cattle shed, he'll meet you there."

"Good to see you again, Seb," said Caleb. "And thanks for the information. We'll have to talk over the weekend." He looked worried.

Seb nodded. "That'll do," he said. "See you later, Vinnie! Enjoy the rest of the show." He smirked.

"Uh, Seb!" Lavinia called.

He looked back.

"That way," she said, pointing the opposite direction.

"Why don't you just walk me back?" he asked, slightly mischievously.

Lavinia glanced at Caleb and bit her lip.

Seb laughed and walked off in the direction she had pointed.

"Where's Vinnie?" Matt asked as Seb met him in the shed.

"She's still looking around the show," Seb replied.

"On her own? Or has she met up with someone she knows?"

"Yes, she's with someone," Seb answered vaguely.

Uncle Matt shook his head. "I suppose it's Caleb," he said. "He's a good fellow, and I'd be very happy if something came of their friendship, but not for a few years yet."

They loaded the heifer into the trailer and set off for Cherryhill.

"Did you enjoy the show?" asked Uncle Matt as they drove out the gate and onto the road.

"I did," replied Seb. He laughed. "I never thought I'd see the day!"

"I'm sure!" Matt laughed as well. "Your expectation of your time on a farm has been completely turned on its head."

"And I thought I was coming to a weird, religious family, who never smiled and were pretty much stupid because they ignored science!"

Uncle Matt smiled sadly. "I'm afraid that's what a lot of people out there think. They just don't realise that true science is totally compatible with the Bible. So many great scientists believed in God. I was reading the other night about the way that Christianity caused so many people to investigate science. C.S. Lewis said something along the lines of 'Men investigated science, because they expected laws in science, and they expected laws in science because they believed in a lawgiver.' Men like Isaac Newton, James Simpson, Louis Pasteur. We'd be much worse off today if those men hadn't discovered what they did."

"We were never told that these men believed there is a God," remarked Seb.

"I can believe that," said Uncle Matt. "Atheism is shouted from the rooftops, but people get angry when Christians try to speak up. I'm glad you're having the opportunity to see things from a different perspective and getting the opportunity to think for yourself. Atheists accuse us of brainwashing our children, but they fail to recognise that that's exactly what they are doing to so many of the young people today."

Seb nodded. "They really do," he said. "It's so clear to me now that there is a God. I can see the evidence all around."

"But you do remember, Seb, that even though you believe in the existence of God, it doesn't make you any better than the atheists."

Seb looked at him, puzzled. "What do you mean?" He was surely better than the atheists, who didn't even believe God existed.

"Do you know we are all born sinners? God has a standard, and we can never, ever measure up."

"But I'm not a bad person, Uncle Matt. I've made mistakes, but I'm not a *sinner!*"

"The Bible says that there is no difference, that all have sinned and fallen short of God's glory."

"Even you?"

"Especially me, Seb! Don't you remember the story I told you about my friends being killed? I was rebelling against my parents and God. That was sin. And I still sin. I try not to, but Christians aren't perfect either. We should try our best, and we have the Holy Spirit to help us, but we won't be perfect until we reach heaven."

"And Christians are people who have trusted the Lord Jesus Christ?"

"That's right, Seb! Well remembered! It's only those who are saved – who have trusted the Lord Jesus – that will be in heaven. Those who have not trusted Him will be in hell."

"But that seems really unfair! 'Believe in Me or else I'll send you to hell!' "

Uncle Matt shook his head. "Firstly, we deserve judgement because of our sins. And secondly, people *choose* to go to hell. God has offered them a way to be in heaven. He gave His only Son – He could give no more – so that people could be in heaven. If they reject God's provision they themselves have chosen to go to hell. And it's eternal punishment: it will never, ever end."

Seb was silent for a moment. Uncle Matt slowed to a stop as the traffic lights turned red.

"But why does trusting in Jesus make the difference?"

"Because He died for our sins. He took the punishment, so we can go free. When we trust Him our sins are fully forgiven. The Bible talks about our sins being removed as far from us as the east is from the west. Do you know how far apart east and west are?"

Seb thought about it. "If we went east, we'd just keep going round the world and we'd never start going west!"

"That's right," replied Uncle Matt. "It's an immeasurable distance. And so it is when we trust Christ – God removes our sins so far from us we'll never meet them again!"

Seb thought about that. Was he a sinner? He thought about the things he had done, things which, deep down, he knew weren't right and made him feel uneasy. Things like stealing, using bad language, getting angry, thinking wrong thoughts. Not to mention the time he crashed Uncle Matt's truck. Yes, he had to admit he probably was a sinner. But bad enough to go to hell? He wasn't convinced.

Chapter Nineteen

"Well, well, well, this is a nice surprise!" Madge bustled around the kitchen, making tea and carrying mugs and buns from the pantry to the table. "I thought ye'd forgot all about us, Lavinia!"

"I was busy with the heifer," Lavinia explained.

"Aye, I heard that!" replied Madge. "And I gather ye did right and well! Second place, was it? That's no tae be sniffed at! But what's all this I hear about you goin' about the show wi' a young man! You're far too young tae be courtin'." She shook her head disapprovingly.

"I'm not 'courting', Madge," Lavinia protested.

"Hmm! That's no what I heard. If ye don't want rumours tae be spread, well, ye better take care no tae start them! But I suppose ye could dae a lot worse than Andrew Harvey's wee fella. They're a right family, wile polite, and Andrew's done well for himsel'. If that young boy, what's he called – Cable, isn't it? Well, he's... Hey! What are you lot laughin' at? Matt?!" She swung round to look at Matt, who quickly became engrossed in the Farming Times paper spread out on the table. He looked up after a few seconds, face arranged into a solemn look. Only his eyes were laughing.

"It's Caleb, Madge," he replied.

"Sure that's what I said," she exclaimed. "Cable!"

Seb gave a snort of laughter, which set Lavinia off. Tommy gave a chuckle, and Uncle Matt's straight-faced efforts crumbled.

Madge stood with her hands on her hips and frowned at them all. Lavinia bent over, clutching her stomach. "I… I'm s-s-sorry, Madge," she wheezed. "But it's Caleb, not C-c-c…" and she began to laugh again.

"I still don't understand what you're laughin' at. That's what I said, and anyway…" She dashed over to the stove, throwing her arms in the air. "Oh dear, this tae will be stewed. Right, sit over. I baked a rhubarb tart this mornin'. I've more rhubarb than I know what tae dae with. Tell Karen tae come round anytime and take as much as she wants. I hate tae see it goin' tae waste, but me and Tommy can't eat it all. It gives him bad guts anyway. He's tried all sorts o' things and nothin' helps. That wee man down beside Freddy Robertson does herbal stuff. All these wee potions and powders. They're s'posed tae work, but I dunno. I'll maybe have tae give them a go sometime. I've a wile sore toe, ye know. Oh boys, sometimes it's pure agony. I think it's come fae that time I…"

"Madge! MADGE!"

"Hey, what? What? Oh, you're ready tae eat. Right, Matt, sure you give thanks for the food."

Matt thanked God for the food and had barely said 'Amen' before Madge began to talk again.

"Where was I? Oh, aye, my toe. My shoes rub on it somethin' awful and it leaves it all red. One time it got that bad that it went all red and yellow, and this disgustin' oul pus started comin' out... "

"Madge!"

"... It was just rotten! Ye should have seen the sight o' it, all swollen and beelin'... "

"MADGE!"

"Hey? What now, Tommy?"

"I don't think these young ones want to hear about your toe while they're eatin'."

Madge looked at Seb. "Right enough, son, ye look a bit pale on it. Are ye feelin' all right?"

Seb nodded.

"Ye know, there's a wile bug goin' round at the minute. It lands ye in bed and ye're there for days. Vomitin', diarrhoea, the works. I hope tae goodness ye don't have that!"

Seb was beginning to feel progressively queasier the longer Madge talked.

"Did you hear that Freddy Robertson had cattle stolen on Tuesday night?" asked Matt, taking pity on his squeamish nephew.

"Oh, aye, I heard that. That's too bad. It just makes me *mad!*" she exclaimed, pounding her fist on the table and making the mugs and plates jump. "It's no in the slightest bit fair. Them boys need stopped, or they'll be the ruination o' all the beef farmers in the area. It makes me sick tae think o' them rakin' in all that money that they never worked a day for in their lives."

Seb had to agree. It wasn't fair and it was time they were stopped. And the perfect opportunity was fast approaching. They needed to speak with Caleb soon.

"Caleb is so glad you overheard those men at the show," Lavinia said. They were walking down the back lane on Saturday afternoon to bring the cows up for milking.

"I'm sure he is," replied Seb. "I hope that finally we'll be able to stop them once and for all."

Lavinia stopped dead. "Did you just say 'we'?"

"Yes," said Seb, nodding. "Sure you want to be a part of this?"

"A part of what, exactly? You do know that Caleb is for housing his cattle that night in the shed closest to the house. I think he'll likely stay up just in case, but they'd never be able to get them out of the shed without the whole family waking up. And they have sensor lights and CCTV around the yard too."

Seb shook his head. "But, Vinnie, this is our opportunity! We know they'll be at Caleb's on Monday night. This is our chance to stop them once and for all!"

Lavinia shook her head. "But, Seb, how many do you think there are?"

Seb tried to think. "I think I heard four different voices, and they talked about 'the Chief'."

"So there could be at least five strong men. Three of us could never stop them. The idea is crazy!"

"But you haven't heard my idea yet!" Seb protested. "Go on, just text Caleb and tell him we need to talk to him."

Lavinia looked at him dubiously. "I'm not sure about your bright ideas," she said.

"Well, then I'll stop them myself," he said. He wasn't sure how that would even be possible, but he was hoping the thought of him attempting something like this would convince Lavinia to help.

"No way!" she exclaimed. "That's the stupidest idea I've ever heard!" She shook her head and pulled her phone from her pocket. "I'll see if he's free after dinner this evening."

Seb looked away and smiled smugly. He'd figured right this time!

"I don't see why we can't just tell the police what you heard." Caleb wasn't budging. He was determined to lock his precious animals safely inside.

"They'll not believe me!" Seb explained again, sitting on the top bar of the gate to one of the fields. "And even if they did, do you really think they would hang around a dark field all night waiting for the rustlers to come?"

Lavinia scrunched up her nose. "He's right about that, Caleb," she said.

"Well, I don't see why I should risk my cattle," he protested.

Seb sighed, frustrated. "Caleb, it's like this," he explained. "I only heard them by chance. I don't know who they are, where they usually meet, or anything else. All I know is that they are planning to steal your cattle on Monday night. That information is priceless. We need to *act!*"

Caleb's shoulders slumped. "Tell me again why we can't ask Dad or Matt for their advice."

"We just can't," he said. "You know they will want to do it the proper way, phoning the police, and, like I said, that just won't work. Sure we can manage on our own anyway!"

Lavinia was listening to the conversation, looking from one to the other. "I think we need to do this, Caleb," she said.

"You do?" he asked, surprised.

She nodded. "You know that if we don't help out, he'll try it himself, and we'll be worse off."

Caleb shook his head. "Okay," he conceded. "But if this goes wrong I'll… I'll…"

"Oh, thank you, Caleb!" Lavinia threw her arms around him.

Caleb looked a bit stunned. "You're welcome," he blurted. "Now, I better get back. I'm supposed to be bringing ice-cream back for the others. Rebekah was getting a bit suspicious."

"Rebekah is my best friend," said Lavinia, "but she's a total wimp when it comes to the dark. She'd be no use at all on Monday night."

"I know," said Caleb, "but I don't know how we can keep it from her. You really should consider telling her. She can keep secrets, you know." He kicked at a stone on the ground to hide his reddening face which, if Seb had been less wrapped up in his plans, might have given him a clue as to the secret Caleb had confided in his sister.

Seb looked at Lavinia. He really didn't know Rebekah, but if she needed to be in on it, that was fine with him.

"Okay," Lavinia said, nodding. "You can tell her, but don't let her talk you out of what we've agreed!"

Caleb shook his head. "This is a totally mad idea, but I've given my word."

Seb smiled. So far his plan had worked. He had both Lavinia and Caleb on board.

They made plans to meet again on Monday evening – a trip to the ice-cream shop after dinner would give them the perfect chance to discuss the plan... and take a drive past Barry's dealership.

Seb tossed and turned. He hadn't wanted to admit to Lavinia or Caleb that he actually hadn't been able to think of a suitable plan yet. How could three teenagers, four if you counted Rebekah, ever manage to stop a number of strong men?

He stretched his hands behind his head. His mind turned to Barry. He was convinced that he was involved in some way. Seb was one hundred per cent certain that the Ranger had been used at least twice for previous thefts, but Barry maybe had had enough when it came back with the wing mirror damaged. What had they used lately? He wished Cherryhill Farm was closer to town, at least close enough that he could keep an eye on Barry's vehicles. Seb sat up in bed. Now, that was an idea that just might work! But could he persuade an already reluctant Caleb to try it? He really hoped so.

Chapter Twenty

Seb watched the pups feed from Jess. They were a week old and growing rapidly. Their eyes were still closed, but they were starting to pull themselves around by their front legs. Jess allowed him to stroke them, although she watched protectively over them. Lifting them out to be weighed alarmed her, and she didn't relax until they were all safely back nestling close to her belly.

The little runt was growing, but he hadn't yet caught up with his brothers and sisters. He often got pushed out of the way when they were feeding. Seb felt a bond with the tiny dog – he knew what it was like to be small and forgotten. He hoped Uncle Matt would keep the pup, but Lavinia said that he was more likely to keep one of the strong, lively pups instead.

Seb heard footsteps crunching on the sawdust, which had been trailed out towards the shed door, and turned to see Aunt Karen approaching. She peered into the enclosure and smiled at Jess and her seven little pups.

"They're growing so quickly," she said softly. Jess lifted her head at her voice and gave her tail two thumps on the ground.

Seb nodded. "I'd never seen such young pups before," he said.

Aunt Karen smiled. "There are a lot of things you hadn't seen until you arrived here!"

Seb had to agree.

"Are you enjoying yourself, Seb?" asked Aunt Karen.

He nodded. He truly was enjoying himself. In fact, if he was pressed, he'd have to say he was as happy as he'd ever been – much happier than he'd ever been back home.

"That's good," Aunt Karen went on. "I thought it would all work out eventually and you would settle in here. Your mum really misses you."

Seb looked at his aunt. He hadn't known that she kept in touch with Mum. Or that Mum even thought much about him. He had to admit to himself that he didn't think much about her. In fact, he tended to block out all thoughts of home. They didn't make for warm and cosy feelings.

Aunt Karen sighed. "Your mum has had a hard time," she said. "She made some bad choices when she was younger, and has lived with the consequences ever since."

Seb didn't want to ask what the choices were. He figured hooking up with his dad had to be one of the worse choices his mum had ever made. But if she hadn't, he wouldn't have existed. His stomach twisted. That wasn't a nice way to think of your existence – as a product of bad choices.

Aunt Karen squeezed his arm. "What is it, Seb?" she asked.

"Oh, nothing," he said, shrugging.

"Was it something I said?" she pressed, looking troubled.

Seb bit his lip. If he denied it, she wouldn't believe him. "I was just... Um..." He took a deep breath. "It was just what you said about Mum making bad choices. It just occurred to me that if she'd made good choices, I..." He swallowed. "I wouldn't be here," he ended quietly.

"Oh, Seb!" Aunt Karen exclaimed. "Oh, I wasn't meaning that you were a consequence of bad choices! Yes, your mum would have had less pain had she not made the choices she did, you know that, but please don't think for one moment that you aren't meant to exist. God knew what your mum would do, He knew about you and He created you. He loved you before you were ever born. He has a purpose for your life. You know, God is God. We can make choices and decisions, and God lets us make those choices because we have our own will, but, at the end of the day, nothing happens outside of His knowledge and control."

A purpose! God loved Seb, personally, and had a purpose for his life? "What kind of purpose?" he asked, amazed.

"Well, firstly, God's desire is that everyone should be saved. And when we get saved, it is God's purpose for us that we live for Him. God has different things for each Christian to do. Some move to other countries and spend the rest of their lives telling others about Him. Some spend all their days where they were brought up, like Tommy, who lives an honest, godly life in his simple way. But wherever we are, being a Christian gives us something to live for - a purpose to life."

Seb thought about that. He longed to have a purpose to his life. He was enjoying his time at Cherryhill. Here, he felt there was some purpose – he could help on the farm. Try to stop the cattle rustlers. But in a few weeks he would have to go home, and he was dreading it. The thought of going back made him feel as if he was being smothered in a thick, dark blanket. If there was ever anyone who needed a purpose to life, it was Seb.

Rebekah sneaked a glance across the aisle at Seb and Lavinia as they were singing the first hymn. She seemed to be sending an unspoken message – one full of nervous excitement and fear. Seb looked down at his hymnbook. If she wasn't careful Uncle Matt and Aunt Karen would figure out something was up. Caleb seemed to be tense as well, standing too straight, shoulders squared. Goodness, did these people never have any excitement?

Seb was unable to concentrate on what the preacher was saying. His mind was full of plans and possibilities. This time tomorrow he would need to have every detail arranged. The others were depending on him.

"Now is the day of salvation!" The preacher leaned over the side of the desk. "Young people, we can't offer you salvation tomorrow. Anything could happen. God only guarantees it today!"

The words broke through Seb's cloud of plans. He bit his lip. He was too busy. And, after all, nothing had happened to him yet. He would think about God's salvation when the rustlers were safely behind bars, he promised.

"You're going where?" Aunt Karen asked, frowning.

"To get ice-cream with Rebekah and Caleb again," replied Lavinia, trying her best to look as innocent as she could.

Aunt Karen looked towards her husband. "Matt?"

Uncle Matt rested his Bible on his knee. "I'm not sure about this, Lavinia," he said. "You didn't know when to come home the last time."

"Oh, Dad!" Lavinia pleaded. "We'll be home whenever you say, I promise!"

Matt and Karen exchanged another look.

"Well, okay," he said. "But you need to be home at ten thirty. No later."

Lavinia flung her arms around her father. "We will!" she called, and dashed from the room.

"I thought we weren't going to be able to come tonight," Seb commented as they headed towards the town.

"Yes," added Lavinia, "they only agreed on the condition we're home no later than ten thirty."

Caleb smiled. "They're not risking letting you out without a curfew this time."

"That's all very well and good, but how do you intend to sneak out later tonight?" asked Rebekah, looking worried.

"I have no idea!" declared Lavinia. "I just hope Seb has a good plan up his sleeve!"

Seb said nothing. He thought his plan was brilliant, but he just had to get the others to agree.

"What is your plan, Seb?" asked Caleb.

"We're nearly at the shop. I'll tell you then."

Lavinia took a large spoonful of her strawberry cheesecake ice-cream and closed her eyes in bliss. "Mmm, this is good!"

"Sally's has the best ice-cream in the world," proclaimed Rebekah.

Caleb shook his head at his sister. "I don't know how you would know," he said. "You haven't exactly travelled too far!"

Rebekah frowned at him. "When you taste the best, you don't need to try anything else to prove it. And this is the best. Therefore we don't need to prove it."

Seb and Caleb exchanged amused glances at her logic.

"Okay, Seb," Caleb said, changing the subject. "Run us through your plan."

Seb swallowed his mouthful of mint choc chip ice-cream. "Right, here's what I thought," he began. "I don't know what time the men will be arriving, but I imagine it's going to be sometime after most people go to bed. We'll need to sneak out after our folks are all asleep."

"Hold on a minute," interrupted Rebekah. "That's not going to work. Mum isn't a good sleeper and she wakes up with the slightest noise. There's no way she's not going to hear us leave the house."

Seb turned to Lavinia. "What about Uncle Matt and Aunt Karen?"

She shrugged. "I think we could manage it," she said. "As long as we can get down the stairs without them creaking, we'll be safe enough. But how do we get over to the Harveys'?"

"Hold on, I'm coming to that," Seb told her. He turned to Caleb. "Is there any way you can sneak out?"

"I can climb out my bedroom window," he replied.

Rebekah's mouth dropped open. "Caleb, that's not safe!"

"It's fine," he replied. "I've done it before. It's the only way to get out, as Dad has so many sensor lights at the back of the house. My room's at the front," he explained to Seb, "and there's a floodlight shining on the front of the house all the time. Mum and Dad's room is at the back. Unless Mum goes to sit in the living room and happens to pull back the curtains and look out the window, she won't know."

"But I can't do that!" exclaimed Rebekah.

"Why not?" her brother replied. "Your bedroom is right beside mine and you have the porch roof right below it. I can't believe you haven't even thought of it before!"

Seb looked at Rebekah. Her face was turning white at the thought.

"Look, it's okay, Rebekah," he said. "I've something in mind that you can do without having to leave the house."

The colour began to return to her face and her shoulders slumped in visible relief.

If that was how scared she was about climbing out a window, there was no way she could have handled the rest of the evening.

"So, once we get outside, undetected, what then?" asked Lavinia.

"Okay, this might be a little more complicated, but Caleb has to come and get us."

Caleb shook his head. "You're right, Seb. It is more complicated. I can sneak out of the house, but there's no way Mum isn't going to hear the car leave the yard, especially with the muffler on the exhaust."

Lavinia and Rebekah looked at each other and giggled.

"Any other vehicle you can take?"

Caleb frowned. "The quietest car is Mum's, but she keeps it in the garage. And the garage is at the back of the house, so that's not going to work either."

They were silent for a few moments.

"Caleb, do you remember the old car you kept down at Calum's granny's house?" Rebekah asked.

Caleb laughed. "I'd almost forgotten about that car! Good thinking, Rebekah. Only..."

"What is it?" asked Seb.

"It's an old car one of my friends and I had for rallying around the fields. Mum and Dad never let me have one, so when I got it I never told them. They never did find out!"

"I wonder if it's still there," said Rebekah.

"I'm sure it is," replied Caleb. "And Granny Tiernan is as deaf as a post, so she'd never hear a thing." He winced. "The only problem is that it's neither taxed nor insured. And there are hopefully going to be police involved somewhere in this operation..." He raised an eyebrow at Seb, who nodded. "So, I could get into big trouble."

"It's okay," Seb reassured him. "You just need to pick us up and take a trip into the town."

"What?!" exclaimed Lavinia. "I thought you wanted to catch the rustlers."

"I do," said Seb. "But I'm convinced they're using Barry's vehicles."

"But you said they didn't always use the Ranger."

Seb nodded. "Yes, but I still think they are using his vehicles. And they've used the Ranger a lot; they might use it again."

Rebekah looked at him, puzzled. "But, Seb, I don't understand what you want to come into town for."

"Okay, here's the plan. Caleb picks us up, takes us to Barry's. We'll call there on the way home now and check it out. Hopefully it'll be obvious which vehicle they're using. We'll watch for them and when they leave – I assume they'll need to go and get a trailer – then we'll go back to Caleb's field and wait for them. They've driven right into the field at least once before so we need to make sure the cattle are at the far side of the field. When they drive in, we shut and padlock the gate."

"That won't stop them," laughed Lavinia.

"No, but it'll slow them," retorted Seb. "Caleb, can you get us a padlock?"

When Caleb nodded, Seb continued, "And then we call the police. Hopefully they'll come very soon, but if not, we track them and keep letting the police know."

Caleb looked dubious at the plan. "And hope they don't happen to notice the lack of tax and insurance of the car," he muttered. He looked worried. He was risking a lot for this venture.

"And what do you want me to do?" asked Rebekah.

"You keep your phone nearby; we need someone on standby to report our movements to… just in case… "

"Just in case what happens, Seb?" asked Lavinia, beginning to look anxious.

"Oh, nothing will happen," he assured them. "It's just for peace of mind. It'll work out perfectly. Rustlers arrested, no more cattle theft. And everyone will think we're great. You'll see!"

Chapter Twenty-One

The last of the ice-cream was scraped from the paper tubs and the young people made their way to Caleb's car.

"So you want to snoop around Barry's yard?" Caleb asked Seb.

"Not snoop. Investigate," he replied.

"Same thing," Lavinia retorted.

They made their way across town to the dealership. As before, it lay silent in the semi-darkness. Caleb pulled into the same lay-by, this time at the end where the trees hid the car. They made their way across the road, over the low wall and into the yard.

"Do you see the Ranger?" asked Rebekah.

It wasn't in the prime place where it had been parked on previous occasions; instead, a grey Golf GTi was being used to lure potential customers. Caleb stopped to admire it.

"If I ever earn enough money, I'm buying one of these," he said, to no one in particular.

Seb was scanning the yard – no Ranger to be seen. He made his way towards the wall behind the office. "Caleb," he called.

Caleb looked up. Seb waved him over. "Help me up this wall again," he said.

Caleb sighed, but joined his hands together for Seb to put his foot on. He sprang up onto the wall. As before, the sensor light came on.

Suddenly, he heard Lavinia hiss at him. "Get down, Seb, someone's coming."

He glanced around to see headlights coming down the road. He could hear the engine slowing as it approached the dealership. He took one quick look into the yard and jumped back down. There had been no sign of the Ranger.

"Quick, we need to get back to the car," said Rebekah. Her eyes were wide and she was beginning to look pale.

Caleb shook his head. "No time," he said. "If we make a run for it, we'll definitely be spotted. Lean against this wall. Hopefully they'll not come round this side."

"What about the sensor light?" whispered Lavinia.

Seb shrugged. Hopefully the person hadn't noticed it.

The four of them crouched against the wall, where it joined another wall at the back of the property. They hoped the blue Peugeot parked in the corner would hide them. After what seemed an age, the sensor light blinked off.

The vehicle stopped on the road and they heard the rattle of chains as the gate was opened. The car door slammed and the vehicle drove into the forecourt. They held their breath.

Seb could feel Rebekah trembling next to him. She was clutching Lavinia's arm.

The creak of the large gates indicated the person, whoever it was, was moving into the yard. Footsteps moved in their direction, and stopped just on the other side of the wall. Rebekah grabbed Seb's arm with her other hand, and clung on for grim death. Seb winced.

The person cleared his throat. They heard the rattle of keys in the back door of the office and the *beep beep beep* of the burglar alarm. The beeping stopped and the door closed again.

"I think it's Barry," whispered Seb.

Lavinia leaned across Rebekah and nodded.

They froze as the door opened again. The footsteps shuffled off. Soon they heard the door to the shed being slid back and a vehicle starting.

"I bet that's the Ranger," muttered Seb.

The vehicle was driven out of the yard. It came closer to where they were hiding and turned in the open space between the rows of cars. They pressed against the wall as the headlights suddenly lit up their hiding place. Rebekah whimpered.

"Don't move," hissed Caleb.

It pulled in front of the office and the door opened, then slammed shut. Seb waited for the feet to move around the corner, but the footsteps moved away from them, towards the gate to the yard instead.

"That was close," whispered Lavinia.

They listened as the shed was locked up, the office door opened and the alarm set, the door and the yard gates locked. The car started and drove out of the yard, engine idling as he relocked the main gate, then moved off slowly in the direction he had come from.

As the car moved out of sight, Rebekah slumped to the ground. "That was the scariest experience of my life," she cried, putting her head in her hands. Her long, blonde hair fell forward. Lavinia rubbed her back.

"You did well," she encouraged.

Caleb cleared his throat. "We really better go. We've only ten minutes to get back to Cherryhill."

"Oh no," Lavinia groaned. "We'll never make it home in time."

They staggered to their feet and ran to the car. Seb stopped at the wall and looked back. Sure enough, the Ranger was parked, ready for the rustlers, he assumed.

"I'm sure he's left the key somewhere," he said.

Caleb shook his head. "No, Seb, we need to go. If we're late, Matt and Karen will be really suspicious and your plan for later will be scuppered."

Seb took one more look at the Ranger. There seemed to be a tarpaulin covering something in the back. He longed to go back for a look, but he needed to stay on the right side of the others. He stepped into the car.

"I can't believe Barry didn't see us," Lavinia commented on the way home.

"How do you know it was Barry?" asked Rebekah. She was still trembling, but looked like she was beginning to recover from her ordeal.

"I would recognise that deep, chesty throat-clearing anywhere," replied Lavinia. "He's a smoker, and always has loads of phlegm in his throat. It's disgusting! But how come he didn't see us?" she asked.

Caleb was whipping round the bends at a remarkable speed, trying to get home by Lavinia and Seb's curfew. "He was likely looking behind him or looking in his mirrors to reverse at that point," he said.

"I don't think he has the best eyesight," remarked Seb. "I noticed that he's always narrowing his eyes to see better."

"Whatever it was, I'm just glad he didn't," sighed Rebekah. "And I'm glad that I'm doing nothing scarier than standing by the phone later."

Seb had to agree. Rebekah was a stunner, but she wasn't exactly going to make a great heroine anytime soon.

They made it back at 10:32pm. Uncle Matt and Aunt Karen were just heading to bed and were gracious enough to overlook the two minutes.

Seb made his way to his room. Setting the alarm clock for 12:55am, he got ready for bed and pulled back the quilt. As he was about to turn out the light, he caught a glimpse of the black Bible on the dresser. He hadn't thought much about it these days, but he would, he promised, once these rustlers were safely dealt with.

He needn't have worried about setting the alarm. He tossed and turned. Every time he began to drift off to sleep, he woke with a jolt, scared of sleeping through the alarm and missing the excitement. He ran through the plan once more. His jeans and sweatshirt lay at the end of the bed. He would get up and pull them on, meet Lavinia at the top of the stairs. They would creep down as silently as they could and make their way outside, stopping to pull on their boots. Caleb would be waiting for them just a few field lengths from the top of the lane. Then they'd make their way to Barry's dealership and wait for the rustlers to appear.

If it worked, it was a good plan. But any number of things could go wrong. Matt and Karen might hear them leave. Caleb's old car might be gone. The rustlers might see them following them. The police might not come in time. They could lose track of the rustlers completely and they might make off with Caleb's cattle after all. Seb hadn't admitted it to the others, but he was nervous. He wished it was one o'clock already so they could put their plan into action.

Beepbeepbeepbeepbeepbeep... Seb sat bolt upright in bed and fumbled for the alarm. After knocking it over, he finally managed to get it switched off. His heart thumped. He hadn't realised it had such a loud, shrill tone, and knocking it over didn't help. He listened for a few seconds. All quiet.

He stepped out of bed and pulled on his jeans and a black sweatshirt.

Rummaging around, he finally located his socks – one near the door, the other almost under the bed. He pulled them on and tiptoed to the door. Turning the wooden knob, he pulled open the door. Good. It didn't creak. He closed it gently behind him and padded along the hall. Lavinia was waiting outside her room. She gave him the thumbs up and began to pad down the stairs.

Creeeak! They froze and waited. The house remained silent and Lavinia moved off again. Seb avoided the step. Lavinia paused near the bottom, pointing at the last step. "Don't step on that one," she whispered. "It creaks the worst of all." She stepped over it and Seb followed. He was horrified when he caught his foot and started to fall. Grabbing Lavinia's arm, he managed to steady himself but banged his arm against a brass umbrella stand at the front door just as the grandfather clock began to chime. Lavinia put a hand over her mouth. Seb quickly held his hand against the stand to reduce the ringing sound. Upstairs they could hear the creak of someone rolling over in bed.

"Quickly," Lavinia mouthed, tiptoeing towards the back door.

Once outside, they breathed a sigh of relief.

"I thought for sure we were found out," Seb whispered.

"Me too," replied Lavinia. She glanced at her watch. "Caleb should be here by now."

They walked silently up the lane. So far, so good.

But the night had only begun.

Chapter Twenty-Two

"Where is he?" Lavinia looked anxiously at the glowing hands on her watch. "We've been here almost fifteen minutes."

Seb shrugged. "Maybe he couldn't get out of the house when he wanted to."

Lavinia pulled her phone from her pocket and pressed a button to illuminate the screen. "He hasn't been in touch. Should I phone him?"

They heard a car in the distance. "What kind of car will he be driving?" asked Seb.

"Um, a grey one," Lavinia answered.

"Yes, but what make and model?"

Lavinia bit her lip. "I don't actually know," she admitted. "I never took much notice when we were at Granny Tiernan's."

Seb shook his head in disgust. Lavinia was usually very clued in for a girl, but not when Caleb was around.

The car lights shone around the bend. Seb and Lavinia pressed against the hedge. The car rattled to a stop and the window was cranked down. "Hey, you two! Sorry I'm late, it took me a while to get this old girl started," Caleb called. "Hop in!"

Seb got into the front seat. Lavinia was struggling with the back door. "Oh, sorry, Vinnie," Caleb called. "That door doesn't open. Come around this side."

Lavinia climbed in and they sped off. "This isn't the way to the town," said Seb.

"Nope," said Caleb. "But we need to turn around and the only place is either at the end of Matt's lane or Tommy's lane. We'll take the next wee road and that'll swing us back onto this road at the side of Cherryhill nearest the town."

Seb looked at his watch. It was now 1:30 and they wouldn't be at Barry's until 1:50 at this rate. "Caleb, change of plan!"

"What?" Caleb's head swung round to look at him and the car wobbled.

"Watch the road," called Lavinia from the back.

"I don't know what time the rustlers are intending to meet at, but I think someone should stay at the field to watch for them."

He could detect Caleb shaking his head in the dim light. "Seb, I really don't like that idea. What if they do turn up? One person on their own; it's not safe!"

"But all we'd have to do is just watch and phone for the police. I'll stay."

"Well, why don't we all go there instead of going to Barry's?" asked Lavinia.

"Yes, isn't that a more sensible suggestion?" Caleb added.

Seb groaned. Why on earth would these people not trust him? They were making it very difficult. He took a breath. "No, some of us need to be at Barry's, so we know exactly which vehicle they're using. Then you should follow it, at a distance, of course. If we know they're coming we'll be better prepared and can even phone the police before they arrive."

Lavinia scrunched her nose and shook her head. Seb's logic wasn't making much sense to her. "Why can't we just phone the police now?"

"Because we've no proof yet!" said Seb, exasperated.

"But following a pickup truck along a road isn't exactly proof either," Lavinia pointed out.

Seb ignored her. She didn't know what she was talking about. "Caleb, leave me off at your farm," he said.

"Are you sure?" Caleb asked.

"Totally," replied Seb. "The two of you can head to Barry's and follow them back. Just make sure you keep your distance. Turn off your headlights if you can get away with it. And keep me informed."

"Um, Seb," ventured Lavinia. "How do you propose we do that? By telepathy?"

"Oh." Seb had forgotten he was phoneless.

"Why don't you take my phone, Seb?" offered Caleb. "You need a phone more than I do. Vinnie has her phone anyway." He reached into the side pocket of the door and handed Seb a gleaming, latest model iPhone. "The passcode is 2580."

Chapter Twenty-Two

Seb's eyes widened. "You're lending me this?"

Caleb nodded. "Take good care of it, won't you?"

"I'll guard it with my life," he promised.

Caleb chuckled. "I'd prefer you don't die over the head of a phone. Just don't do anything daft with it."

They were driving along Caleb's road. The house lay dark and quiet. Caleb's mum didn't appear to be spending a sleepless night downstairs anyhow. Caleb slowed. "Okay, Seb," he said. "You see this field on the right? This is where the cattle are. I've five in the field and I put their feeding trough right at the bottom these past few days. I'm hoping that when they see the men coming, if they aren't already at the bottom of the field, they'll assume they are going to be fed and head there. That'll give you as much time as possible to lock the gate." He fished in his pocket. "Here's the padlock. I think you'd be best locking them in as soon as you can. We'll have to put the car into a gateway further on down to hide it, so we'll be a few minutes."

Caleb seemed to have thought through and planned for situations that Seb had never envisaged. As he climbed out of the car, and Lavinia took his place in the front seat, he wondered if he was really up to this task. But this was only a precautionary measure, he told himself. The others would let him know the rustlers were coming and they'd be close behind. He wouldn't be alone for long.

Seb shivered. The wind had picked up and he wished he had remembered to lift his coat on the way out the door of Cherryhill farmhouse. He was crouched behind the hedge, just inside the gateway of the field across the road from the scene of the impending action. He had no idea how long he could be waiting here, and the minutes were dragging past. Suddenly he felt a vibration in his pocket and pulled out Caleb's iPhone. A text message from Rebekah: only two words. 'What's happening?'

Seb figured he may as well reply – it wasn't like he didn't have time. 'It's Seb. I'm waiting at the field in case they turn up. Caleb and Vinnie are going to Barry's. Caleb…'

He froze. He could hear an approaching vehicle. It came closer, but didn't slow, and instead sped past. He returned to the text message. '…Caleb lent me his phone. I don't have one at the minute.' He added a sheepish-looking emoticon and sent the message.

Setting the phone down, he stood up and stretched. His leg had gone to sleep and he wiggled his foot to get some feeling back. Sitting down on the cold ground, he glanced at his watch. The luminous hands showed it was 1:50. Caleb and Lavinia would be at Barry's by now, surely. Maybe he should phone them and see if all was going according to plan. As he reached for the phone, he heard the sound of another approaching vehicle. He strained to listen above the sound of the increasing wind. It came closer, but instead of continuing along the road, slowed to a stop just on the other side of the hedge from Seb.

He could hear the rattle of the empty cattle trailer. His heart started to pound. This was it. But where on earth were Caleb and Lavinia? They wouldn't have had time to get to Barry's and back. He hoped they'd hurry back when they saw the Ranger was gone.

He heard the door open and close, then the bar pushed back to open the gate. A slight creak as it was swung back on its hinges and the vehicle moved through the gate into the field. Seb could hear the gate being closed while the vehicle idled, the door opening and closing again and then the bouncing and creaking of the trailer as it was pulled over the bumpy, rutted field.

This was Seb's opportunity. He leapt to his feet and quickly climbed the gate onto the road. He crossed the black strip of tarmac and reached for the padlock in his pocket. He paused. What benefit was there to padlocking the gate? The police would never be able to drive right out here before the men were ready to leave, and the padlock would advertise to the rustlers that someone was watching them. That was all very well if Caleb and Lavinia were there too and they had a car to make an escape if needed. But to lock the men in the field when he was here on his own...? He shoved the padlock back into his pocket.

He could see the side lights of the truck further down the field. Caleb's cattle had stayed at the bottom of the field, as he'd hoped. Seb could hear the sound of the bellowing cattle and just about make out their dark shapes. Should he go closer? He wasn't sure how many men there were, and while he assumed they were using the Ranger, he hadn't seen it. Surely it would be better having more details for when he phoned the police.

Seb made his way around the perimeter of the field, keeping close to the hedge, knees bent, ready to freeze at any moment. As he drew closer, he could make out two men, rounding up Caleb's cattle. Seb felt a surge of anger welling up inside him. They were taking them all! How dare they?!

He crept forward. He could now make out the truck – it was the Ranger, shiny and pristine. It was parked towards the side of the field, using one of the gates of the trailer to prevent the escape of cattle through the gap between the trailer and the hedge. Seb slipped between the Ranger and the hedge and peered through the bars of the gate. The men were trying to herd the cattle towards the trailer as silently as they could. Four of the cattle were complying; the fifth, a lighter coloured one, was skipping off to the far corner of the field.

"Just leave him," he heard.

"Are you sure?" a second voice replied. "He's the best one, in my opinion." Who was that? Seb was sure it was the same familiar voice he'd heard at the show.

"Let's get these on first, and we'll give it another go."

Seb stepped back from the gate as the men herded the cattle on the trailer. He melted against the hedge as they moved the side gate into place. His palms were damp and his heart was pounding again.

He needed to hide. The men were trying to round up the last animal. They wouldn't be staying here much longer. Would he have enough time to get back to his original hiding place before he was spotted?

Footsteps thudded closer and the gate was pulled back again. As the animal's footsteps clattered up the ramp into the trailer, Seb's eyes widened in horror. He was trapped! In a few seconds the driver would come around this side of the truck and trailer, and he'd be spotted. He put a foot onto the wheel of the truck, ready to launch himself into the open back of the truck, when he felt someone catch his arm.

Chapter Twenty-Three

Seb wheeled round, fists raised, stifling a scream.

"Rebekah?" he whispered, puzzled. His arms dropped to his sides.

He heard the tailgate swinging up and being secured. Time enough later to figure out how and why Rebekah was here in the field, instead of standing by the phone in the safety of her bedroom.

"Get in," he hissed, gesturing to the back of the truck. She shook her head.

"You've no choice," he mouthed. "They're coming!" He swung himself up and reached down for her. She landed beside him and he pulled the tarpaulin over them just as the men walked past. Two long objects, like sticks, landed on their tarpaulin-covered legs. Seb winced. That hurt!

The doors slammed shut and they moved off. He could feel Rebekah trembling beside him. "What are we doing here, Seb?" she moaned. "And how are we ever going to escape? I hate your ideas!"

Seb took a deep breath. There had been no other option, but he had no clue how they would get out of this sticky situation.

The jeep and trailer bumped up the field and stopped briefly. The gate opened, they drove through, and waited on the gate being secured. In a few moments they headed down the road.

Seb pulled the tarpaulin down slightly. It smelled musty and they were all jumbled up with random pieces of farming tools.

"How did you get to the field?" he asked his nervous companion.

"I climbed out the window," she said, bottom lip trembling.

"You did?" Seb asked, astounded.

She nodded. "I had no choice," she said. "Lavinia phoned to say they had broken down near Barry's. They walked the rest of the way, but the Ranger was gone. She tried phoning you, but you didn't answer. Then I tried, but I couldn't get through either. The only way was to go and tell you."

Seb's heart sank. The phone! He checked his pockets – not there. He shook his head. He had left it down beside him when he was waiting and had forgotten to lift it again.

Rebekah shivered. "I've never been as terrified in my whole life."

"You did well," Seb encouraged her. He really hoped she had more courage than she thought. The night was far from over, and the other two weren't going to be able to help now.

"What about phoning the police?" she suggested.

Seb groaned. In all the excitement he had totally forgotten about that part of the plan. "Go ahead," he told Rebekah.

She pulled the phone from her pocket and began to dial 999. "Oh no!" she exclaimed, frantically pressing buttons.

"What is it?"

"The battery! This phone is so old; the battery doesn't hold its charge anymore." She pressed the little button to restart it, but it died after a few seconds. Further attempts were less successful – the screen remained black.

"What do we do now?" she asked. Even in the darkness he could see the fear in her eyes.

Seb looked away and bit his lip. "It'll be fine, you'll see."

She turned to him, anger rising. "How do you know? This was a stupid, crazy plan. I wish I'd never agreed to have anything to do with it." Her voice had risen.

"Sshh! They'll hear us."

Rebekah dissolved in tears.

Seb put his head in his hands. This was a crazy idea. He was really starting to regret this. But there was no way to turn back time. He was going to have to make the most of it. How could he get them out of this tricky and dangerous situation?

The vehicle slowed and turned down a narrow road. They had been driving for half an hour. The road surface was no longer smooth and even; instead it was bumpy and full of potholes. Seb figured they were likely across the border into the Republic of Ireland by now. He knew that more than two men had agreed to be part of the operation, so he guessed that the others were at a changeover stop.

They slowed further and turned into an even bumpier lane. They jostled about in the back with the miscellaneous tools. "Ow!" Rebekah rubbed her head where she had hit it against the edge.

They felt the vehicle slow again and Seb pulled the tarpaulin back over them again. "Just follow me here," he said in a low voice. Rebekah began to tremble again.

"You're fine!" Seb told her. "You've been brave tonight. Everything will turn out, you'll see."

A dubious sniff was the only answer.

They could feel the stones crunching beneath the tyres, as they pulled into what they assumed was a yard. They reversed a short distance and the truck pulled to a stop. The doors opened and closed as the men got out. Seb could hear the low voices of another two men greeting them. The doors to a shed rolled back and the voices moved inside. Seb peeped out from under the tarpaulin. A light was shining from the shed.

"Quick, all clear," he said as he nudged Rebekah to climb out.

She shook her head. "Where are we going?"

"Just get out," he said urgently. "This stuff in the back must be things they need, otherwise they wouldn't have brought it. They're going to come back any minute."

Rebekah stood up on wobbly legs.

"Stay low," Seb hissed. "If they look out, you'll be in full view."

She sat on the edge and swung her legs around, then dropped to the ground. Seb followed.

"What now?" she asked, rubbing her arms.

Seb paused. Only one thing occurred to him. He opened the truck door and climbed in.

Rebekah watched him, eyes wide. "What are you doing?"

"Get in! Hurry!"

She paused, then obeyed his instructions.

Seb turned the key and the truck roared to life. He put it in first gear and moved off. The trailer felt like it was dragging him back. There wasn't a moment to lose.

A glance in his wing mirror showed the silhouette of four men running out of the shed. Seb plunged his foot on the accelerator. The truck and trailer bounced violently on the rocky lane.

Suddenly, a deafening *boom* sounded.

Rebekah screamed. "They're shooting at us!"

Seb clutched the steering wheel desperately and concentrated on getting to the road as fast as he could.

Rebekah sat crouched over, her head in her hands. Then she reached down and lifted a dark wood and metal double-barrelled shotgun. Seb's head whipped around to look at her.

"Look at what I've found," she told him.

"I've never used one before," he admitted.

"I have," she said, holding the gun across her lap. "Dad has one similar to this and he taught us how to shoot. He wanted us to know how to handle a gun safely."

"Well, maybe you better use it!"

"What?"

Seb could see the headlights of the other vehicle coming down the lane. They reached the bottom and swung onto the narrow road. Seb planted his foot on the accelerator and tried to avoid the potholes as best he could. He felt sorry for the cattle in the trailer. The other vehicle was gaining on him.

"Be ready to use that gun, Rebekah," he told her.

"But I don't want to kill anyone!" she protested.

"Well, just scare them then!"

She flipped a small lever and the gun opened in half to reveal a circular brass cap of a cartridge in each of the chambers. "It's loaded," she told Seb, as she closed it up, then proceeded to open the glove compartment. Empty, apart from a small cardboard box. She opened the box – it was full of cartridges.

They'd reached the end of the road. He tried to remember whether they had made a left or right turn into the road. He chose to turn right. The heavily loaded trailer was slowing him up and the other vehicle was rapidly gaining.

"Time to show off your skills, Rebekah," he told her, willing the Ranger to build up speed.

Rebekah put down her window and turned round, leaning slightly forward, left knee resting on the seat, right leg straight and braced against the glove compartment. She aimed a few metres above the approaching vehicle and fired. Seb could see the vehicle's headlights wobble slightly.

"Good girl, Rebekah," Seb said. "That has unnerved them."

Finally, the speed was building up. He concentrated anxiously on the road. The last time he drove at great speed in a borrowed pickup truck, it had all ended very badly. He hadn't had time to put on his seatbelt, and Rebekah had taken hers off to fire the gun. He was speeding along an unknown road, no idea where they were, with gun-wielding angry cattle rustlers on their tail. They didn't even have a working mobile phone between them. Another loud *boom* sounded from the vehicle. Great. Now they were shooting at them. And Seb wasn't convinced that they had the same reluctance to kill as Rebekah had. "Go again, Rebekah," he said.

Again, she opened the window and fired, aiming her shot above the vehicle. She had barely pulled herself back in the window when another louder *boom* reverberated. Seb jumped and the truck wobbled dangerously from side to side, the movement made worse by the heavy trailer behind.

"Look out," screamed Rebekah, as the truck wavered onto a grass verge and skidded towards a green hedge. He tried to steer the truck back towards the road, but it was out of control. The only thing he could do was to slow as much as he could before he hit the hedge. As the hedge loomed closer, Seb closed his eyes. He heard the crunch and crash of the branches above Rebekah's screams as they ploughed through, scattering leaves as they went. The trailer bounced violently along behind them. Finally, they slowed to a stop.

He looked at Rebekah. She was deathly pale and breathing heavily. "Are you okay?" he asked.

She nodded weakly. "I... I think so," she replied, her voice shaky.

Seb could hear shouts growing closer. Seb leaned his head against the headrest. This was it. He had failed. There was no point in trying to outrun the men – they would only shoot them. He took a deep breath. The driver's door was yanked open. Rebekah cried out and fainted, slumped against her door.

The barrel of a shotgun was pointed straight at him.

Chapter Twenty-Four

"Don't move, or I'll shoot," a low, mean voice came from the darkness beyond the door.

Seb raised his trembling hands slowly above his head, as he'd seen in films.

Another voice emerged from the darkness. "Hey, Kevin, they're only kids!"

Two frowning faces appeared in the doorway. The gun lowered.

"What are you doing?" asked the bearded man, Kevin, angrily. "Why are you interfering in our business? And how did you..."

The younger man poked his head around Kevin. "Is the girl all right?" he asked. Rebekah was still out cold.

Seb nodded. "She just fainted when she saw the gun."

"Who shot at us? You didn't shoot and drive at the same time?"

Seb jabbed a thumb in Rebekah's direction. "It was her," he replied.

The younger man let an appreciative chuckle out of him. "Brave girl!" He looked at her unconscious form with interest.

Kevin frowned. "Get the gun, Tony!" he snapped. "We don't want any more stupid actions from these daft kids."

Tony walked around the Ranger and opened the passenger door. He caught Rebekah as she began to fall out and pushed her head forward onto her knees. He located the gun on the floor and lifted it out. As he slammed the door, Rebekah stirred. As she groggily sat up, she spotted Kevin looking in the door and her eyes filled with horror and fear. Kevin's lip curled in disgust. "Right, Tony," he snapped. "Get the girl and I'll take the boy. This is a serious mess they've left us in. Phone the others and get them here as soon as they can. What the Big Chief will say is more than I know," he muttered, grabbing Seb's arm and hauling him from the truck.

Kevin led him roughly to the gap in the hedge and waited for Tony to catch up. He was taking his time with Rebekah, guiding her along with one arm around her shoulders, the other hand around her upper arm. Seb frowned. He felt sick that his actions had caused Rebekah to be landed in a dangerous situation when she had no desire to be anywhere other than sleeping in her bedroom in the middle of the night. And now for her to be the focus of a sleazy, greasy criminal...! Not for the first time that night, Seb wished he could turn back time.

It was dark and silent in the back of the jeep. Seb braced himself against the side as they made their way around bends and over bumpy roads. He didn't know where they were taking them. This had turned out to be the worst decision of his entire life, and now they were trapped. How would they ever escape? What would these men do to them? He had heard stories of people who had disappeared without trace. Would he and Rebekah just be added to the statistics, or was there any hope of them being able to go home?

A sniffing sound came from beside him. He reached out a hand and awkwardly patted Rebekah's arm. "This is a nightmare," she wept.

"I know," he replied. "I'm sorry," he added, softly.

The jeep bounced and rattled. "I think we're going back to the shed," said Seb. What would happen to them there? He was filled with dread.

They pulled into the yard and the back doors were opened. They were marched into the shed and a length of rope was produced. Kevin tied Seb's hands together behind his back and made him sit along the wall. The ground was dirty with cattle manure and the corrugated tin had gaps where a cold breeze blew through. He then tied Seb's feet together and proceeded to tie Rebekah's hands and feet. He wrapped two lengths of rope around a wooden beam and attached them to the ropes around their feet. Then they left, turning off the light, pulling the doors shut behind them. Seb heard the click of a padlock.

Time dragged in the darkness of the shed. This night seemed to be lasting forever. He twisted his arms, but the ropes were tight and only chaffed his wrists. He wondered what would happen when the men came back. Would they shoot them? Or torture them to keep them quiet, then let them go? No one would ever think to look for them here, away in the wilds of Ireland, miles from anywhere. He hoped by this stage Caleb and Lavinia would have realised they were gone and alerted their parents. He groaned. What would Uncle Matt think of him? Taking his pickup truck for a joyride was mild compared to the dangerous situation he'd landed them in now. Why hadn't he listened to the others when they thought it was a crazy idea? Could it be that he was trying to win their approval? To prove he was a good person? But surely his motive was faultless.

"Rebekah, if you do something bad, but your reasons for doing it are good, surely that counts for something?"

Rebekah gave a short laugh devoid of humour. "Seb, we're tied up in a shed, I'm terrified that we're going to be killed and you're wanting to justify getting us into this situation! You are... are... " she spluttered, "unbelievable!"

Seb sighed. Obviously his good motives didn't count for anything with Rebekah anyway.

"Are you saved, Rebekah?" he asked.

There was silence, then a quiet, "Yes." Another pause, then, "Why do you ask?"

Seb shrugged, forgetting that it was dark and she couldn't see him. "Just wondering," he replied.

They sat in silence for a while, then Rebekah began to speak. "I'm sorry, Seb. I got saved when I was seven, thinking over the verse

I'd learned in Sunday school – 'Christ died for our sins according to the Scriptures.' I realised that He had died for me and I put my trust in Him." She sighed. "I've just realised that I haven't been a good example of a Christian tonight. I'm sorry."

Seb blinked, confused. "What do you mean?"

He could hear her shifting around, trying to find a more comfortable position on the cold ground. "I've been giving in to fear," she replied quietly. "There's a verse in the Bible which says, 'I will trust and not be afraid.' So I've been wrong in giving in to fear. God knows we're here and He's with me."

"But what if… if we are… killed?" Seb finished softly.

Rebekah let out a trembling breath. "I have to be honest and say I don't like that thought," she admitted. "I don't like the thought of being in pain but at least if I'm killed I know for certain I'll be in heaven. I'd rather not die, all the same!"

"Me neither," admitted Seb. Where would he be if he died? He knew it wouldn't be heaven. There was only one other place, and that was hell. He did not want to be in hell. But that was where he deserved to be. He could see it now. He had sinned. He had done wrong. He had denied the existence of God. He had broken His laws. He had assumed he wasn't bad enough to go to hell. He had rejected God's Son. And before the morning dawned, he could be in hell. But was it too late for him? Would God save someone who came running at the last minute?

"The blood of Jesus Christ His Son cleanses us from all sin," whispered Rebekah.

"What did you say?" Seb asked. He'd heard that before! It was a verse from the Bible.

Rebekah repeated the verse, "The blood of Jesus Christ His Son cleanses us from all sin."

All sin? Even Seb's rebellion and wickedness? Could it be that the Lord Jesus Christ's death on the cross was enough to save Seb? To make him fit for heaven?

Seb no longer had any doubts about the reality and existence of God. He was firmly convinced that the Bible was God's word to mankind. And if God said it, it had to be true! Nothing else could cleanse him from sin but the blood of God's own Son. Seb let go of his own efforts. Christ died for him!

"I'm saved!" he exclaimed. He felt as if a heavy weight had been lifted from him, a weight he'd been carrying around for years. He was going to heaven, cleansed from his sin!

"You're saved?" asked Rebekah. "When did you get saved?"

"Just there now!" he replied. "After you repeated that verse."

Rebekah gave a faint laugh. "I was repeating it for myself; I didn't even think you'd heard me until you asked what I'd said!"

Seb gave a laugh of delight. "What's the hymn about power in the blood?" he asked. "I heard it when I first arrived at Cherryhill and it made no sense to me then."

Rebekah began to sing:

> "Would you be free from your burden of sin?
>
> There's power in the blood, power in the blood!
>
> Would you o'er evil a victory win?
>
> There's wonderful power in the blood."

Seb joined in softly in the chorus:

> "There is power, power, wonder-working power,
>
> In the blood, of the Lamb,
>
> There is power, power, wonder-working power,
>
> In the precious blood of the Lamb."

They sang it over and over until Seb knew each line by heart. He felt he was about to burst with joy. They no longer thought about their situation, tied up in a draughty shed, uncertain of their fate.

Rebekah giggled.

"What's so funny?" asked Seb.

"I was just thinking of Paul and Silas in prison in Philippi in the middle of the night, singing hymns to God. We're singing in prison too!"

They could see faint light shining through the cracks of the shed.

"It must be getting light outside," Seb commented.

"The men will be back soon," Rebekah said. Her voice was calm.

"Let's pray and ask God for help," suggested Seb. "The God Who can save me from hell can certainly preserve our lives."

Rebekah nodded. "If it's His will," she added, then bowed her head and closed her eyes. Seb followed suit and began to speak to

His heavenly Father, the One Who loved him unconditionally, Who would never let him down and would always be with him, right to the end.

Chapter Twenty-Five

Seb jerked awake. What was that noise? And where was he? Why couldn't he move his arms?

As he looked around, he remembered. They had been tied up in a shed by cattle rustlers after hiding in the pickup truck and then trying to escape with it. And Seb had got saved last night. Hadn't he? Or was it just an emotional experience brought on by the adrenaline of their adventure? Suddenly, the words of the verse flashed through his mind. *The blood of Jesus Christ His Son cleanses us from all sin.* He felt an assurance deep in his soul – he was cleansed from all sin.

Rebekah stirred beside him and opened sleepy eyes. A strand of blonde hair had fallen over her face and she jerked her head to flip it out of the way.

They heard the crunch of a vehicle on the stones, then the sound of another vehicle and trailer pulling into the yard. Seb and Rebekah looked at each other.

"I will trust…" whispered Seb.

"…and not be afraid," finished Rebekah, a nervous smile on her face.

The men were back.

"Well, you two," the shed door was pulled back and Kevin entered. "How did you sleep?" He laughed, a harsh guffaw devoid of humour.

He walked to where they sat and looked down at them, a sneer on his face. "I admire your courage, but it's landed you in hot water. You should have left well enough alone. No one meddles with us and gets away with it. I think we need to teach you two a lesson." His eyes glinted with an evil gleam.

He grabbed Seb's arm roughly. "Up!"

Seb staggered as the rope attaching him to the wall pulled taut. Kevin pulled out a penknife and slashed the rope. "Tony!" he called.

Tony sauntered into the shed and over to Rebekah. Pulling out his own penknife, he cut the rope tied to the shed, and pulled her to her feet. Her legs gave way and she sank to the ground. "What's wrong, beautiful? Gone all weak at the knees at the sight of me, huh?" He laughed long and loud. Rebekah ducked her head, but not before Seb saw her lips move. *I will trust and not be afraid.*

Tony lifted her and slung her across his shoulder, one arm behind her knees. Kevin trailed Seb out of the shed, his tied feet making walking almost impossible. Seb blinked as they stepped out of the shed into the early morning daylight. As his eyes adjusted, he spotted the jeep, and, off to one side, the Ranger, dirty and scraped, a wingmirror casing hanging off, but still with the trailer attached. A loud bawl let him know the cattle were still there. They'd had a rough night as well.

Two figures stood beside the cattle trailer. Seb bit his lip. Four strong men against two teenagers. They didn't stand a chance. He glanced at the men. And stopped dead. Kevin dragged him forward and he stumbled. He struggled to regain his footing and glanced across again. He couldn't believe his eyes. Standing against the cattle trailer was someone Seb knew. Someone he had trusted.

It was Joe.

Seb and Rebekah were once again bundled into the back of the jeep. The cattle trailer was reversed to the shed door and the cattle unloaded.

"Did you see Joe?" asked Seb.

"Who?" asked Rebekah. "I saw nobody, the way that slimy creep had me over his shoulder. I wish he would keep his hands off me."

"Joe - Uncle Matt's farmhand. He's one of the men in this operation. I thought the voice was familiar, but I couldn't place it. I can't believe that he's a criminal! And to steal cattle from people he knows!"

"Why didn't you say anything?"

"I don't know," Seb replied. "He gave his head a tiny shake and I missed my chance. He might be our only hope. I've always got on well with him. He's been living a lie, though."

They watched out the back window as the men exited. As they stood in a cluster in the yard, Joe turned round and kicked at a stone. He looked towards the jeep and mouthed, '*Trust me.*'

Chapter Twenty-Five

Seb frowned and turned to Rebekah. "Did he just say 'trust me'?" he asked.

Rebekah nodded. "Yes, but he hasn't exactly proven himself trustworthy."

They watched as the knot of men broke up. Kevin and Tony walked towards the jeep, while Joe and a fourth man got into the Ranger and headed down the lane.

"I'm getting really scared again," admitted Rebekah.

The men got into the front and started the engine.

"We're taking you on a roadtrip, kids!" Tony laughed.

The jeep moved off down the bumpy lane, and onto the road. "Do you recognise this place?" asked Seb, in a low voice.

Rebekah shook her head.

They turned right onto a better maintained road and Seb watched with interest. This was the way they had driven last night in their wild chase with the rustlers. Soon they passed the large gap in the hedge which they had ploughed through. He looked at Rebekah and grinned sheepishly. They had obviously had trouble recovering the Ranger and trailer from the field, if the mud tracks were anything to go by.

The road began to narrow and climb a winding path up a steep hill. Halfway up, Seb noticed a large drop to the right side of the jeep into a deep valley below. He shivered. He had had no idea last night where this road led, and had they not ended up in the field there was every possibility they'd have ended up rolling into the valley. They wouldn't have survived. He breathed a prayer of thanks to God for His preservation of them.

Over the hill, they began their descent, through wild brown rushes and heather. The land was barren and empty; there were no houses in sight. Except for one. A small abandoned stone cottage stood in the middle of a field a few hundred metres away. The jeep slowed and turned in a rough lane, knee high grass growing down the middle.

The cottage was in even worse repair than it had appeared to be from the road. What was happening?

They pulled in front of the house and the men got out. Opening the back door, they pulled Seb and Rebekah out and steered them to the house. It was dark and smelly inside and a cloud of flies whizzed past Rebekah's head. She screamed. The men laughed. "Only a few flies, precious," Tony said, in a mock-soothing voice.

"If that's the worse you'll face today…" began Kevin.

They laughed. Seb shivered. How could men be so wicked?

"See, we're taking good care of you," said Tony, pointing to two bottles filled with a dubious-looking liquid, and a packet of biscuits on the windowsill of the one small, boarded up window. "And we're not even tying you to anything," he continued. "There's no point. This house may look like it's falling down, but it's more secure than some of them prisons!" The two men looked at each other and laughed. Had these men spent some time in prison to know? Seb wondered. He wouldn't have been surprised.

"Goodbye, my friends!" Tony said, as he stroked Rebekah's face. She jerked her head away and he laughed. "We'll be back later!"

The men walked out of the house and bolted a heavy wooden door behind them. Seb could hear their voices. "I wonder what the Big Chief will want done with them?" Tony said.

"Huh, who knows?" came Kevin's deep voice. "If it was up to me I'd get rid of them. No one would ever find any evidence out here. But he'll have his own ideas..." The voices drifted away.

"I wonder who the Big Chief is," said Rebekah.

Seb shrugged. "Let's pray he has more compassion than Kevin anyway," he said. Then he shook his head. "Any ideas how are we supposed to eat our *kind breakfast* when our hands are tied behind our backs?"

Half an hour later, Seb had figured out how to unknot the rope from Rebekah's wrists. It wasn't easy working back to front, with his own hands behind his back, and the ropes were tied tight. Some light shone from the holes in the roof, but the room was gloomy.

Rebekah wiggled her hands.

"Keep still," Seb told her.

"Sorry! I just can't wait to get my hands free. My arms are in agony."

"Mine too."

The ropes fell from her wrists and she stretched, arms high. "Thank you, Seb."

"You're welcome. Now, do you think you could sort my wrists out?"

Rebekah moved behind him and began to unknot the rope.

"Ow!" she exclaimed.

"What's wrong?"

"I thought I had ripped my nail off," she replied.

Seb said nothing. He couldn't help but think that a ripped-off nail would be the least of their worries before the day was over.

A few minutes later and the rope was off. They both set to work on their feet. It was such a relief to be free. Pulling the packet of biscuits off the windowsill, Rebekah ripped the packaging open. "Pink wafers!" she exclaimed.

Seb grimaced. His least favourite biscuits, but at least it was food.

Rebekah pulled one out. "It feels soft." She held the packet in a patch of daylight and checked the date. She laughed. "They are a whole year out of date!"

Seb shook his head. "So generous, those gentlemen!" he exclaimed sarcastically.

Rebekah giggled and pulled a bottle from the windowsill. She shook it and observed the contents. "Oh, yuk!"

"What's wrong?" Seb took the bottle. The water was a dirty pale brown, and had particles floating in it. He shuddered. "This looks like something that has come from a dirty stream," he said.

"I wouldn't be surprised," said Rebekah, shaking her head. "I'll maybe pass on the water for now, but I'm hungry enough to eat a soft wafer!"

"Me too!" replied Seb. "But we need to thank God for keeping us safe and for providing us with food first."

"Of course," Rebekah smiled.

They managed to consume three soft pink wafers each, then set the packet on the windowsill again. Who knew how long they would be here? Seb didn't think anyone would come until dark.

" 'Men loved darkness rather than light, because their deeds were evil'," quoted Rebekah.

"Those men's deeds are evil all right," remarked Seb.

"I wonder what Joe meant," said Rebekah.

Seb shrugged. "Who knows? He might have been trying to make us think that he would rescue us, just to make us feel better."

"But why did he not let on he knew us? I can't understand it."

"Even if Joe has a plan, he might not get back in time. And how could he fight all those men off single-handedly? They all seem to have guns," Seb replied. "I think we should try to escape. Surely there's somewhere the men have overlooked."

Chapter Twenty-Six

Seb slumped onto the damp floor, dejected. "You'd think that there would be somewhere we could escape," he said.

Rebekah bent down to peer up the wide chimney. She coughed as some dust dislodged. "I can hardly even see daylight up there," she said. "It seems blocked by something."

"Maybe a bird's nest," said Seb.

Rebekah leapt back. "No way! Please tell me you're joking!"

Seb looked at her in amusement. "Are you scared of birds?"

Rebekah scrunched her nose and nodded sheepishly. "I'm scared of most things," she admitted. "Birds, spiders, bats, heights, loud noises..."

"And cattle rustlers," finished Seb.

Rebekah nodded. "I'm not very courageous."

"Well, for someone not very courageous, you're doing rather well."

"I wasn't, until you reminded me that I wasn't trusting in God."

"I didn't exactly remind you..."

"You did, you just didn't mean to."

Rebekah plopped herself beside Seb on the floor. "I kind of wish we could get this over with, and just get home," she said.

"I know what you mean," he agreed.

"Do you think Caleb and Lavinia have told them about Barry?" asked Rebekah, after a pause.

"I hope so, but I'm not sure if they will believe them. They really haven't any evidence to incriminate him, apart from a pickup truck being moved around. They never even saw the Ranger to know for sure that's what the rustlers were driving. "

"And he'll deny everything," Rebekah added.

The hours passed. To pass the time, Rebekah taught him more hymns, until they began to go hoarse.

"All this singing is making me thirsty," said Seb.

Rebekah laughed. "Well, feel free to take a drink! I'll pass this time."

Seb lifted the bottle and screwed the top off. He lifted it to his lips.

"I can't," he said, setting the bottle down.

After another pink wafer they played 'I spy'. There wasn't much in the house to spy, so that didn't last long.

"They'll be eating lunch now," remarked Seb, looking at his watch.

"I'd love a big plate of cottage pie," said Rebekah, her stomach rumbling. "I wonder why no one has come yet. Joe obviously didn't mean what he said."

Seb shrugged. "I suppose we can't depend on men," he said. "I think we should pray again."

They closed their eyes and again pleaded with God to deliver them. They knew it was no trouble to God to do the impossible. And to be rescued from an abandoned Irish cottage in the middle of nowhere was certainly an impossible situation to the teenagers.

Seb listened. The sound of an engine grew louder. Someone was coming. He wished he knew whether it were Kevin and Tony, or their rescuers. He nudged Rebekah, who was curled on her side on the hard ground, asleep.

She opened her eyes and blinked. "What is it? Where am I?" she asked.

"We're locked in the cottage. Someone's coming."

She reached a hand to her head, her eyes squinted in pain.

"What is it, Rebekah?" asked Seb, concerned.

"My head is so sore," she whispered.

Seb felt the panic rising. He desperately hoped these people were coming to rescue them. He didn't know what was wrong with Rebekah, but she didn't look well, and seemed confused.

The vehicle pulled up to the door and he heard the key turn in the padlock.

"So here are our little snoops." A familiar voice snarled. Seb blinked against the bright light shining from the doorway. As his eyes adjusted, he made out the short, stocky form of Barry. Seb was right. He was in the thick of this plot.

Barry moved closer to them and peered down at them. "Huh! It's you again," he snarled. "I should have known you were up to no good, prowling around like that."

Kevin and Tony appeared in the doorway. Barry turned to them. "I knew the Ranger was too easily identified! You should have taken the Defender again, like I wanted you to."

Kevin shook his head. "But Barry, the Defender isn't great with a full load. It can pull it, but it's noisy and slow when we need to get over the border as quickly and quietly as possible."

Barry dismissed their arguments with a wave of his pudgy hand. He squinted at Seb. "Well, we'll not need to worry in future. I'm going to make sure you'll never bother us again." He laughed. Shivers ran up Seb's spine.

"And I see you brought your girlfriend along," mocked Barry.

Rebekah looked up at him in a daze, her pretty face twisted in pain. Barry laughed.

"Right, boys," he clicked his fingers, "this kid needs taught a lesson. Get to it." He turned and strode to the door.

"What about the girl?" asked Tony.

Barry shrugged. "Whatever you want. This one's the ringleader." He pointed to Seb. "She just came along for the ride. Just give her a scare or two, that should be enough. But I don't want that one to even dream of snooping around again. Give him something that'll close his mouth and that he'll never forget."

Seb's heart was thumping in his chest. His palms were damp and his legs were shaking. He swallowed, but his mouth was dry. *Oh God,* he prayed silently. *Help me!*

I will trust and not be afraid, came to Seb. He took deep breaths.

Tony grabbed him and tied his legs together again, then his hands behind his back.

"How did you manage to untie yourself, kid?" he asked.

Seb shrugged.

Kevin produced a long wooden bat and raised it above Seb's knees. Seb closed his eyes and braced himself for the pain.

Suddenly, the cottage door burst open. Two figures, dressed in dark clothes with woolly hats low over their heads, burst in and wrestled Kevin to the ground, tying his hands and feet together. A third grabbed Tony, who had sat beside Rebekah to watch Seb's punishment. Tony kicked out and made contact with his attacker's shin. The attacker staggered and Tony grabbed the bat which Kevin had dropped. He raised it above his head, ready to administer a blow, when one of the other men grabbed his arm. The bat swung dangerously near the man's head before falling to the ground. Grabbing Tony around the knees, they pulled him to the ground and tied him up.

Seb lay in shock. What was going on? They were moving so fast he couldn't see who these men were. One of them pulled off his hat.

Chapter Twenty-Six

"Phew!" he said. "I haven't wrestled like that since I was at school!"

"Uncle Matt!" exclaimed Seb.

Uncle Matt came over to where Seb lay. "Are you okay, son?" he asked. He got out his penknife and cut the ropes. Seb sat up.

"Yes," he replied. He felt an overwhelming sense of relief. He was safe. God had answered his prayer.

Uncle Matt put an arm around him. "We were so worried about you both," he said, eyes damp. "I think we got here in the nick of time."

Seb nodded. "Yes, you did," he replied. "God is an amazing God."

Uncle Matt looked at him with interest. "Seb…"

"Yes, Uncle Matt, I got saved last night."

Uncle Matt threw his arms around him in a bear hug and laughed with joy. "Oh, Seb, that's the best news I've heard in a long time," he said, a huge smile on his face.

A whimper from Rebekah brought Seb's attention back to the present surroundings. He looked over to see Andrew Harvey, her dad, sitting on the ground with his daughter in his arms. He looked over at Matt.

"I don't think she's well, Matt," he said. "We need to get her to hospital as soon as we can. We don't have time to wait for an ambulance."

Matt stood up and walked over to where they were sitting. Rebekah was deathly pale and wasn't moving. Andrew gathered her up and began to walk to the door. Matt and Seb followed. He noticed the third man, sitting off to one side. Joe! He had come through on his promise after all. He nodded to Seb. "I'm glad we got here in time," was all he said.

Andrew lifted his daughter into Matt's jeep and fastened her seat belt. He moved around to climb in beside her. Seb went to sit in the passenger seat.

"Hold it right there," came a mean voice.

Seb's heart sank. Barry. He hadn't left. They looked to where he was standing, at the side of the house. He was pointing a shotgun directly at them.

"Come on now, Barry, you don't want to fire that gun," Uncle Matt told him.

"Ha, don't I?" He raised the gun in the air and fired. The sound reverberated around the hillside.

"What would you gain? You know they'll find you."

"Not if I leave the country. I've made enough money to live comfortably for the rest of my life. I might go to Argentina. Or Columbia. Or..." The gun lowered slightly.

"Maybe Venezuela?" ventured Matt.

"Too dangerous." He shook his head and the rolls of fat around his jaws swung from side to side.

"Mexico?" asked Uncle Matt. Seb could see movement in the corner of his eye at the door of the cottage, but he forced himself not to look.

Barry cocked his head to the side. "I like that idea, Matt. You always were a sensible fellow. Good beaches, tequila, big parties..." The butt of the gun now rested on the ground and he had a slight smile on his flabby face.

Joe moved silently behind Barry. Barry seemed to have been transported to a powder-white beach, tequila in hand.

Joe kicked the gun from Barry's grasp and pulled Barry backwards. Seb dashed to the gun and grabbed it.

"Careful, Seb," called Matt.

Seb handed the gun to Matt, who opened it and removed the cartridges.

Barry could move faster than Seb thought and drove a large fist into Joe's nose. The blood gushed and Joe staggered back. Before Barry reached his fist back for another punch, Matt had grabbed the large arm. Between them they managed to pin him to the ground, just as the first Garda Síochána car made its way up the grassy lane. Seb sighed in relief. Finally, the police had arrived and they could leave.

As they drove down the lane and onto the winding road, Seb looked back. He hoped justice would be done. They would be required to give statements to the police on both sides of the border, but, for now, the priority was to get Rebekah well again. He closed his eyes and began to pray. He thanked God for their deliverance, and asked Him for Rebekah's recovery. Then he fell asleep.

Chapter Twenty-Seven

Aunt Karen had prepared a large pot of stew and baked a loaf of wheaten bread. After a diet of soft pink wafers, the beef, carrots and potatoes tasted better than anything Seb had ever eaten before. The family looked exhausted, but very relieved.

"I'm so glad you're back with us, Seb," said Aunt Karen, smiling. "We were terribly worried."

"I nearly died when we eventually got back to Caleb's and you weren't there. And then when we discovered Rebekah was missing…!" Lavinia threw her hands in the air.

"How did you get back?" asked Seb.

"Well, the car broke down just before we reached Barry's, so we walked the rest of the way. And then we saw the Ranger was gone. That's when we tried to phone you."

"But the men had already arrived and I'd left Caleb's iPhone in the field," said Seb, sheepishly.

Lavinia rolled her eyes. "I knew Caleb shouldn't have given you his phone. Anyway, he found it when we were looking for you. We'd rather have found you, but I'm sure he's glad now he has his iPhone back intact. Then we phoned Rebekah instead and finally persuaded her to go and find you." She shook her head. "We thought she would find you near the entrance to the field. I can't believe you went right down the field beside the Ranger."

Seb bit his lip. "I thought I'd better check it was the Ranger before I phoned the police. And when you weren't there I thought putting the padlock on would only make them realise someone had found them out and we weren't ready for them to know yet."

"So we tried to push the old car," went on Lavinia, "but no amount of pushing would work. Then when we tried to phone Rebekah again there was no reply. That's when we really started to worry."

"And that was the first we knew that you'd left the house!" exclaimed Aunt Karen. "It was a massive shock, hearing my daughter's voice telling me they were stranded in the town because the car had broken down and you and Rebekah were missing!"

Uncle Matt chuckled. "It wasn't funny then, but Karen thought Vinnie had lifted the phone in her sleep and was telling us the details of a bad dream she was having. She told her to go back to sleep, ended the call and only realised it was real when she went to check on her and Vinnie's bed was empty."

Uncle Matt's smile faded. "But it was no dream. What a night we put in. We called the police; we checked everywhere. But you had gone without trace. We told them your suspicions about Barry, but he was nowhere to be found."

"Where did you go?" asked Lavinia.

Seb reached for another slice of wheaten bread and slathered it with butter. "We jumped into the back of the truck and ended up at a shed in the middle of nowhere. I think it's where they leave the cattle, then other people come to pick them up. When the men got out of the truck and went into the shed, we hopped out and got into the cab."

Lavinia groaned. "Don't tell me you took it for a drive!"

Seb nodded.

"What is it with you driving pickup trucks?!"

"It wasn't for fun!" he exclaimed. "It was our only way to escape and get Caleb's cattle back too. Anyway, they started to shoot at us, and Rebekah found a gun and started to shoot back."

"Oh my!" exclaimed Aunt Karen, hand over her heart, eyes wide.

"Oh, don't worry, Aunt Karen, she shot above them. She didn't want to kill them."

Aunt Karen's hands moved to the sides of her face and she closed her eyes. "I'm glad I didn't know what was going on!" she breathed. "A gunfight with criminals! I never thought little Rebekah would do such a thing!"

"Oh, it was my idea, Aunt Karen," explained Seb.

"Ha!" said Lavinia. "That doesn't surprise me. You have the worst ideas in the world, Seb!"

Seb bit his lip. After the past twenty-four hours, he had no option but to agree.

"Go on, Seb," said Uncle Matt patiently.

Seb wasn't sure he wanted to *go on*: the rest of the story didn't paint him in any better a light.

"Well, I crashed through a hedge, then the men opened the door and pointed a gun at us." Aunt Karen grew pale. "Then they hauled us out and put us in the jeep, took us back to the shed and tied us up and left us until the morning." Seb smiled. "But the best thing happened in that shed!"

Lavinia frowned. "What on earth good could happen when you're tied up in a dirty shed?"

"I got saved!" Seb exclaimed, his eyes bright with renewed joy. "Rebekah was quoting verses to herself and I heard her say, 'The blood of Jesus Christ His Son cleanses us from all sin.' I realised that even though I had loads of huge sins, especially being rebellious and putting everyone in danger the way I did, that the Lord Jesus Christ's blood cleanses all my sins. And I trusted Him!"

Aunt Karen pushed her chair back and rushed around the table to hug Seb. "Oh, Seb!" she wept. "That is the best news I've heard in a long time. If that's what God used to speak to you about your need for salvation, then it was worth all the worry!"

Uncle Matt nodded, a smile on his face. Even Martha clapped her hands together and smiled at Seb.

But as Aunt Karen pulled away and went back to her seat, Seb glanced at Lavinia. She was sitting with her head low, biting her lip.

Why, she didn't look happy! He'd thought she would be overjoyed like everyone else!

"So, what happened after that?" asked Aunt Karen.

Seb moved his attention back to Aunt Karen. He'd figure out his cousin's response later.

"They came back in the morning and took us away again in the back of the jeep. That's when I saw Joe and realised that he was one of them."

Uncle Matt shook his head. "I knew Joe's company wasn't great, but I really didn't think that he would have been sucked into criminal activities."

"At least he redeemed himself a bit," added Aunt Karen.

Uncle Matt nodded. "Yes, he came back here as soon as he could and told us what was going on. He thinks he'll be in a lot of bother now for betraying them, but he said he knew what was going to happen to you and he simply couldn't keep quiet."

Seb shuddered. Those men were callous and wicked. "What will happen to Joe?"

"He's going to Scotland as soon as he can. The police need to question him but he hopes that the fact he's helping with their investigation will mean they go easy on him. I've arranged for an old friend there to give him work." Uncle Matt nodded. "He's learned his lesson."

"So they took you to the abandoned house," prompted Aunt Karen.

Seb nodded. "We were there ages, then everything happened at once – the men came back and were just about to beat me up, when Uncle Matt, Rebekah's dad and Joe all came. And then there was Barry."

Uncle Matt shook his head. "Another person I never suspected," he said. "Imagine him being the ringleader of criminal activity!"

"Well, I'm glad you're safe and well," said Aunt Karen. "And Andrew was on the phone earlier. Rebekah was just severely dehydrated, so she's getting fluids intravenously. She's going to be fine."

"What's enter-beansly?" asked Martha.

"Intravenously," repeated Aunt Karen, smiling. "It's where they put a wee needle in your arm or hand and put water in it, so you don't have to drink lots and lots at once."

Martha scrunched up her nose. "I don't like the sound of that!"

Aunt Karen brushed her fingers through the blonde curls and laughed. "Don't worry, pet. You drink enough milk and juice! You don't need intravenous fluids."

Seb pushed his chair back from the table and carried his bowl and spoon to the sink.

"Do you mind if I go and see Jess and the pups?" he asked. "I'll help with the dishes when I come in."

"Oh, don't worry about the dishes, Seb," laughed Aunt Karen. "Go and see the pups, and then you likely should get to bed. You look exhausted."

She was right. Seb did feel as if he could fall asleep on his feet. He pulled on his wellies and walked across the yard to the shed where Jess and her babies were.

As he walked in, Jess looked up and thumped her tail on the ground. The pups were greedily feeding. Seb smiled and watched the sight. He was so thankful to be here, alive and unhurt. He felt that weeks had passed since he'd last stood here – so much had happened.

He heard footsteps and looked up to see Lavinia. She leaned over the partition and smiled at the pups. "I can't wait until they open their eyes," she said.

"Me neither," agreed Seb.

They stood in silence. The runt was pushed away by a big brother and rolled, tiny feet and tail waving in the air. Jess reached out and pushed him back into place with her black nose.

"That one is my favourite," said Seb. "I know what it feels like to be pushed around." He turned to his cousin. "You don't seem too happy that I got saved last night," he said.

Lavinia shrugged, avoiding eye contact. "It's good news," she said quietly.

"So why aren't you happy about it? I thought you'd be delighted."

She dropped her head and sniffed.

A sudden thought passed through Seb's mind. "Vinnie," he began, "aren't you saved?"

She shook her head.

"You're not?" Seb was shocked. He had assumed that she was. She had grown up surrounded by Bibles, had heard preaching since she was a baby... but she wasn't saved?!

"Why not?" he asked, astounded.

She shrugged. "I don't know," she replied quietly. "I just never really thought much about it."

Seb couldn't understand it. He had always been told that Christian parents indoctrinated their children and he'd assumed that Christians' children were Christians too. Of course, he had realised since then that to become a Christian you had to trust Christ for salvation, but he thought that, being brought up in a Christian environment, it would be an easy decision to trust Christ.

Lavinia didn't seem to want to explain her reasons, so he said nothing more. But he would be praying for her.

Chapter Twenty-Eight

"Come in, come in, come in!" Madge held the door open for Matt, Seb and Lavinia on Wednesday morning. "I'm wile glad tae see ye. And I'm glad you're all right, Seb. Goodness me, the fright I got when I heard that you and Andrew's wee lass were missin'. I nearly had a heart attack, so I did." She shook her head and waved them through to the kitchen. Tommy was sitting in his chair, newspaper in hand.

"Matt. Lavinia. Seb." He nodded to each of them, a kindly smile in his washed out blue eyes. "You got the boys, Seb."

Seb nodded. "Well, I found out who they were. But I think it was more that they got me!"

"You were near yoursel', Seb," Madge clucked. "Much as I would have liked tae skelp their backsides, I don't think I'd have gone near them."

Lavinia sniggered.

"And what's so funny, Lavinia?" Madge turned to her, hands on ample hips.

"Oh, nothing, Madge," she said. "I just have a mental image of you sitting with one of the rustlers over your knee, hitting them with a wooden spoon!"

Madge frowned at her, but her mouth twitched. "Wooden spoon, says she!" she exclaimed. "I wouldn't waste a good wooden spoon on those crim-nals! A good sally rod, like my mother used tae use, would dae the trick better than a wooden spoon! Anyway," she turned to Seb, "it was a wile foolish action, what ye did, but we're glad they're caught. Poor Tommy's been livin' in fear o' them comin' back and takin' the rest o' the cattle. Isn't that right, Tommy?"

Tommy lifted one bushy eyebrow. "Well, not exactly livin' in fear, Madge…"

"Close enough!" she retorted. "Anyway, ye can sleep at night now instead o' gettin' up and clatterin' round the house in the wee hours every time a car drives past. I hear ye, ye know!" She wagged a finger at him. "And Cable's cattle are back with him! That's great news. Good they got them traced in time. Once they get them over the border and the ear tags changed…" She pushed the kettle onto the hotplate of the stove and disappeared into the pantry.

Tommy turned to Seb. "Heard you got saved, son," he said, smiling.

Seb grinned. "Yes, I did, Tommy," he replied. "There's nothing like it, knowing my sins are all forgiven!"

Tommy nodded. "Read your Bible and pray, Seb. New believers need to grow."

Madge returned with mugs and plates. "The minurl man was here the other day, Lavinia," she said. "I got a bottle o' thon pineapple stuff. You like that all right, don't ye?"

Lavinia nodded.

"Good. And I've some gypsy creams I baked specially for you, Matt, and german biscuits..." Her voice grew muffled as she disappeared into the pantry and came out with a bottle in one hand and a plate of sweet goodies in the other. "Now, sit over and I'll pour the tae..."

Seb got up from the settee and pulled out a wooden seat at the table. As Tommy gave thanks for the food, and for preserving Seb and Rebekah and saving Seb, Seb found himself strangely moved. He had seldom come across such genuine warmth and care in Belfast and he breathed his own silent 'thank you' to God for arranging the events of his life.

As they stepped in the back door, Aunt Karen appeared from the kitchen with the portable phone to her ear. "It's your mum," she mouthed to Seb. Seb gulped. He wasn't looking forward to having to speak to her. He had let her down yet again. But before he had time to collect his thoughts, Aunt Karen opened the door to the office and handed him the phone.

He took a deep breath. "Hi, Mum," he said, walking in and sitting on the black office chair. Aunt Karen shut the door softly behind him.

"Seb!" came a shaky voice. "Karen has just been filling me in on your latest escapade. What on earth were you thinking?!"

"I don't know, Mum. I wanted to help. But it went wrong again." He swallowed. "I'm sorry."

"Seb, I don't know what to do with you. I don't know whether to be glad you're okay or to be cross with you. Karen said she tried to phone us to let us know you were missing, but I was working night shift and she only got speaking to your dad. He was so drunk he wouldn't listen to her." Mum sounded dejected.

"I'm not surprised," Seb replied. He was glad that Dad didn't know.

"Seb, I've decided I've had enough. I'm moving out. I work to fund his drinking habit, and it's not fair on you, having to live with a monster like that. I should have done it years ago."

Seb lifted the phone away from his ear and looked at it in shock. Mum was leaving Dad?! He didn't think she'd ever have the courage. "But where will you go?"

"I'm looking for a small house, just big enough for you and me. I'm not sure. I haven't told him yet." She sounded terrified.

Seb swallowed. They both knew how he would react to that news. Memories of his dad's drunken rages washed over him and he felt his hands growing clammy and his heart beginning to race. He took deep breaths. A verse Uncle Matt had read this morning flooded his mind. 'Be still, and know that I am God.' God was with him, He knew all about Seb's dad, and He was still in control.

"Did Aunt Karen tell you I got saved?" asked Seb.

There was silence. Then, "What did you just say, Seb?"

"I got saved the other night, while we were tied up in the shed."

"Oh, Seb!" Mum's voice broke and he could hear her weeping. "That's all I've ever wanted for you. I made such a mess of my life and it's too late for me, but that was my only desire for you."

"Mum, the verse that helped me says, 'The blood of Jesus Christ His Son cleanses us from all sin.' If it cleanses from all sin, it's not too late for you."

She sobbed. "Oh, Seb, you don't know what I've done. But I'm so happy for you." She sniffed and her sobs subsided. "I'm not going to tell your dad – he'd only come and take you away, and you need more time with Matt and Karen." She sighed. "I need to go," she said reluctantly, "I'm just on my lunch break and it's almost over. But I'll phone again. Bye!"

"Bye, Mum!" The call ended and he sat, looking out the window, before getting to his knees. He knew that Mum needed God's salvation. She was miserable. He didn't know what she'd done that she thought was so wicked, but he knew that the blood of Jesus Christ cleanses from all sin. God doesn't lie. Then he asked God to save his parents.

Friday night saw Uncle Matt, Aunt Karen, Lavinia, Martha and Seb make the short journey to the Harveys' house for dinner. Seb was slightly nervous. Apart from texting Rebekah to see how she was keeping, he hadn't seen any of the family since their attempt to catch the rustlers. He hoped none of them held anything against him. Uncle Matt had finally given him back his smartphone. "Here you are, Seb," he'd told him. "On one hand I feel I should be meting out punishment for sneaking out and going behind our backs, but I don't think you'll try something like that again!"

Seb shook his head. "Absolutely not, Uncle Matt!" he exclaimed. "And no more driving pickup trucks!"

Matt smiled. "I think you've learned your lesson! But I'd feel a lot safer if you had your phone back. Just in case…!"

"Thanks, Uncle Matt," Seb said. "I don't plan to be in any situations like that again anyway!"

Seb looked out the window at the green fields. The grass was growing again and in another few weeks many farmers would be silaging again.

Matt slowed as they turned into a tarmacked lane. A large house with a front porch came into view. As they drove up, the large wooden door was flung open and Rebekah rushed out, followed by Caleb.

Uncle Matt pulled to a stop. "Hurry up, Seb! Get out!" Lavinia pushed his shoulder.

Seb took a breath and opened the door. Lavinia tumbled out after him and went straight to Rebekah, throwing her arms around her. "I'm so glad you're okay!" she told her.

Caleb nodded at Seb. "Well, Seb!" he said. "Thanks for rescuing my cattle. You nearly got my sister killed, mind you!"

Seb lowered his head. "Caleb, I'm really, really sorry," he said. "And your iPhone…"

"Hey, I'm only joking!" Caleb thumped his arm. "The phone was there, just where you left it. And I'm beyond glad you were both okay.

But see the next bright idea you have?" He shook his head. "I'm telling you 'no' right now!"

Rebekah giggled. Seb turned to see her watching him. They exchanged a knowing look. They'd been through a lot together. She knew what had transpired in the dark, smelly shed. Going after the rustlers was the worst idea he'd ever had, and he'd put a lot of people in danger, especially Rebekah. But during that dangerous experience he had come to know his sins forgiven. His life had been turned round. The emptiness he'd once had had been finally filled. He now had a purpose to his life and a peace that could not be taken away.

As he followed everyone into the house, his eye caught sight of a Bible verse hanging just inside the front door. It was a verse Uncle Matt had read just yesterday morning. Seb had looked it up afterwards in his own Bible and memorised it. It was a verse that had resonated in his being. He had come a long way on his journey – from cynical, unquestioning atheist, believing there was no God, then coming face to face with the unquestionable evidence for God, and finally coming to know Him as the One true God. He smiled, and silently mouthed the words again.

'This God is our God for ever and ever: He will be our guide even unto death.'

Epilogue

The summer had passed in a blur. All the silage was now in, and ready for the winter months ahead. Uncle Matt expected that some of the cows would start calving any day. And Jess's pups had grown into fuzzy, playful black and white rascals. Jess didn't bother much with them anymore, and when she did go in to feed them, they usually jumped over her and swung from her tail. She looked up at Seb, a longsuffering look on her intelligent face as one puppy batted her face with his paw. Seb laughed.

"Poor Jess!" he said. "Don't worry, another few weeks and they'll be gone to new homes."

Apart from one. Uncle Matt had agreed to keep the little runt. He'd shook his head. "No one keeps the runt of a litter, but if that's your choice, Seb, then we'll keep him. Better start to think of a name."

Suggestions had been plentiful. "Bentley," Lavinia suggested.

"Sparky," said Martha.

"Prince."

"Jed."

"Toby."

None were a good fit. It was Rebekah who finally suggested the perfect name. They had ridden their bikes one evening after milking, following a road that meandered through trees and beside streams. After a few miles, they exited onto another road and began to ride up a steep hill. It was a tough climb. As they reached the top, Seb realised that he had been on this road before. It was the way they had come home from the town after leaving Mum back to the train station on Seb's first day at the farm, but a road which they didn't normally use. He stood up to pump his feet on the pedals and finally made it to the top. As he stood breathlessly regarding the valley, stretched out before him, the sun setting behind the distant hills, sky streaked in pinks and purples from an extravagant divine paintbrush, he recalled Uncle Matt's words – "If you want evidence for God, just look at that... It proclaims the existence of a Creator."

"This is my favourite view around here," said Rebekah, who had just made it to the top of the hill. "The glen and the mountains – and just look at those colours!"

Seb laughed. "And not too long ago I thought a big bang formed it!"

Rebekah smiled. "You could call the pup 'Glen', you know. As a sort of reminder of your journey."

Seb smiled. "I like that! A reminder of the God of creation."

Seb picked up Glen and the puppy wriggled. He was almost as roly-poly as his brothers and sisters now, and every bit as feisty. Glen licked his chin and struggled to get down, then ran off to join his siblings. Soon he was in a puppy-fight with his sister. Seb recognised her as Moss, who would be joining the Harvey family.

Seb wouldn't be here to see the pups go. His summer had come to an end, and it was time to go home. Except it wasn't the same home. Mum had finally found a small house for them and had moved out. Dad had phoned Uncle Matt, demanding he tell him where she was, but Mum had cleverly told no one. Not even Seb knew where the house was.

He sighed, thinking back to the phone call. Uncle Matt had refused to let Dad speak to Seb, but Seb had insisted. Now that Mum wasn't there to take the brunt of Dad's anger, he felt the time had come to tell him that he was a Christian. He knew Dad would be angry. But he wasn't prepared for the barrage and volley of foul and obscene language that spewed from his mouth. If he had been in the same room, he was certain he would have been killed. Uncle Matt had grabbed the phone and ended the call. Even Matt looked shaken.

"I'm glad you're not going back to live with your dad, Seb," he remarked.

"Me too!" Seb exclaimed. "I knew he wouldn't like it, but I didn't realise it'd be like that!"

"The man needs our prayers," Uncle Matt had said.

Seb wasn't looking forward to being back in Belfast. Even though he wasn't going to be living with his dad, he didn't know any other

Christians. How would he manage back there, among the old friends and the old temptations? Mum had told him he wouldn't have to change schools. What would Mr Symons say about him being a Christian now? And what if he happened to bump into his dad somewhere?

Glen ran over and began to chew his shoe. What he'd give to stay on the farm for the rest of his life! But the time had come to leave. To step out in faith. To prove God, not only in the good times, but in the bad. Seb had seen the evidence for Him, and believed in Him. Now the time had come to trust Him. For this God – the One Who had created the universe, Who had given men a conscience and morality, Who changed people's lives and gave them something to live for – this God was Seb's God for ever and ever… even unto death.

Bibliography and Further Reading

In writing a book of this nature, it is necessary to use and refer to, in different measures, very helpful books already in print. I would like to acknowledge these sources as below.

*Cargill, Robert W. *Creation's Story*. John Ritchie Ltd, 2008.

*Hodge, B, Mitchell, T and Ham, K. *Answers Book 4 Teens Vol 1*. Master Books, 2011.

*Hodge, B, Mitchell, T and Ham, K. *Answers Book 4 Teens Vol 2*. Master Books, 2012.

Geisler, Norman L and Turek, Frank. *I don't have enough faith to be an atheist*. Crossway, 2004.

Lennox, John C. *God's Undertaker – Has Science Buried God?* Lion, 2007.

Lennox, John C. *Gunning for God – Why the New Atheists are Missing the Target*. Lion, 2011.

Randall, David J (Ed). *Why I Am Not An Atheist*. Christian Focus Publications, 2013.

Strobel, L. *The Case for Christ*. Zondervan, 1998.

Strobel, L. *The Case for Faith*. Zondervan, 2000.

Zacharias, R, Geisler, N (Ed). *Who Made God? And Answers to Over 100 Other Tough Questions of Faith*. Zondervan, 2003.

*Although I would not personally endorse all that is suggested and taught in some of the above sources, for anyone who would like to read more on the subjects of creation, the Bible and Christianity, the books marked with an asterisk are highly recommended and easy to understand.

Scripture References